Border Union Dream

*the inside story of Britain's
boldest railway preservation bid*

DAVID SPAVEN

First published in 2018 by
Stenlake Publishing

54-58 Mill Square
Catrine, KA5 6RD
01290 551122
www.stenlake.co.uk

© David Spaven

The moral rights of the author have been asserted.
A catalogue record of this book is available from the British Library

ISBN 978-1-84033-830-0

This book is sold subject to the condition that it shall not by way of trade or otherwise, be lent, resold, hired out or otherwise circulated without the publisher's prior consent in any form of binding or cover other than that in which it is published and without a similar condition including this condition imposed on the subsequent purchaser. All rights reserved. No part of this publication may be reproduced, stored in a retrieval system or transmitted in any form or by any means, electronic, mechanical or otherwise without the written permission of the publisher.

Printed by
Claro Print,
Unit 2.4, Kirkhill House
81 Broom Road East,
Glasgow, G77 5LL

DEDICATION

Dedicated to the memory of the late Roy Perkins (1946-2015), who deserved a better outcome from his tenacious and visionary efforts for the Border Union Railway Company in 1969-70.

Contents

Introduction	5
1. Before the Border Union Railway Company (BURCo)	9
2. The rise and fall of BURCo	35
3. The lingering death of the railway	101
4. Forty three years later…	135
Appendix 1 – BR freight working timetable 1968-69	137
Appendix 2 – Andrew Boyd's notes of Trip E10, Millerhill-Hawick, 24th March 1969	139
Bibliography and Sources	141
Index	142

Maps

The Waverley Route on 6th January 1969	4
The Carlisle / Longtown area in 1963	50

Photo sections

Four months of vestigial freight from Edinburgh to Hawick	11
Edinburgh to Hawick: a *Mary Celeste* railway	20
Hawick to Carlisle: abandoned to the track-lifters	89
BURCo: its Directors, brand, and sole railway operation	110
Track going, going, gone	113

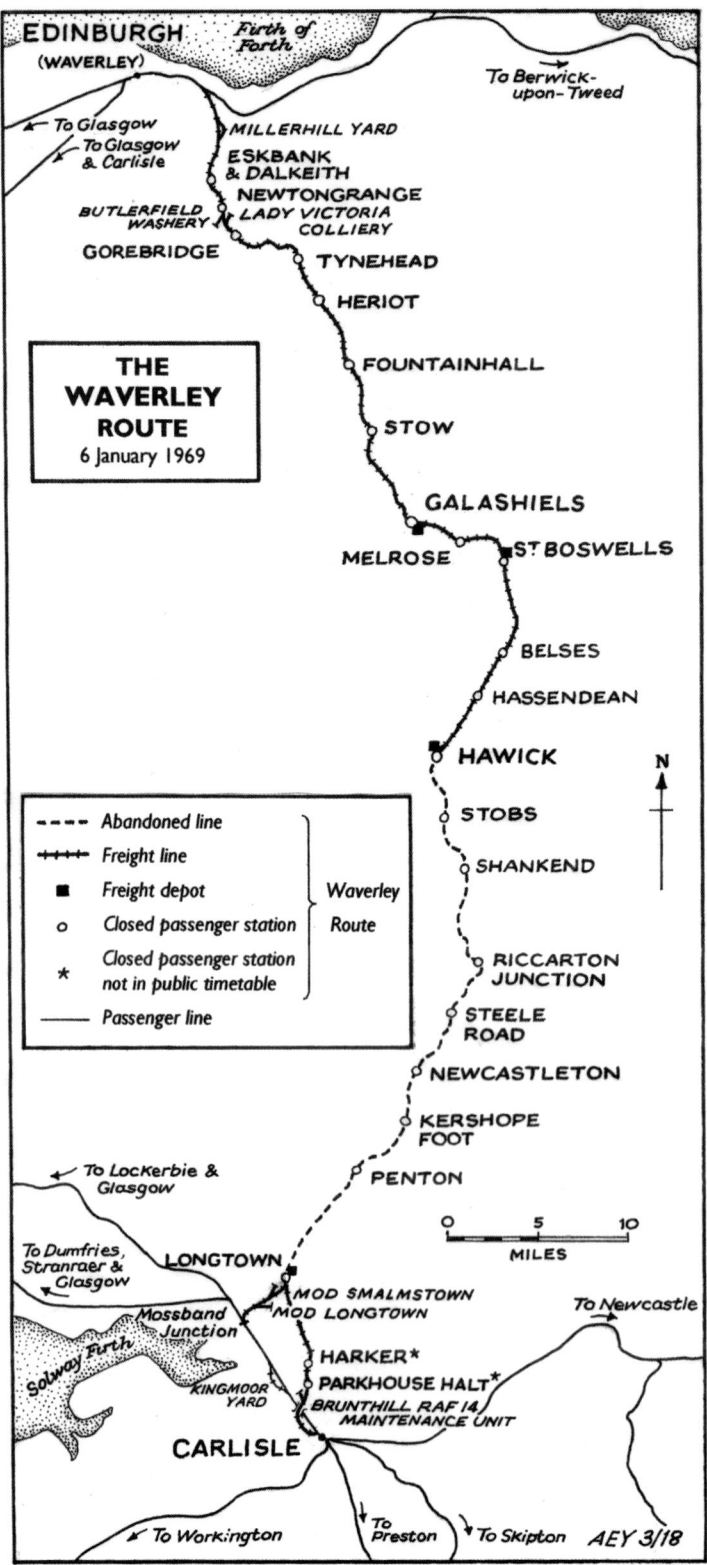

Introduction

The Border Union Railway Company (BURCo) 1969-70 bid to re-open the Waverley Route as a private concern was the most ambitious scheme in the history of British railway preservation – aiming to operate regular passenger and freight trains over the entire 98¼ mile route from Edinburgh via Hawick to Carlisle, following its succumbing to the 'Beeching Axe' on 6th January 1969.

Despite extensive negotiations with British Rail (BR), nationwide networking amongst the 'old boys club' of businessmen and financiers, and dedicated grassroots efforts in the Borders, BURCo failed. However, led by the kenspeckle Bob Symes-Schutzmann – a larger than life character from the TV, rail enthusiast and vintage car worlds – the company and its volunteer support group, the Waverley Association, briefly captured the imagination of the railway world and Borders' folk. Many were left sorely disappointed when the dream crumbled, but the story continues to fascinate railway enthusiasts – and has a wider political and social history resonance.

During my research for *Waverley Route: the life, death and rebirth of the Borders Railway* in 2009-12, I discussed in depth this unique episode in British railway preservation with two of BURCo's three directors: the late Roy Perkins and the late Bob Symes-Schutzmann, and enjoyed unlimited access to the latter's voluminous personal archive. Due to book length constraints, though, I had to edit down the BURCo material from 22,000 words to just 5,000. Now, with the 50th anniversary of Waverley Route closure on 6th January 2019 – and further archive material unearthed – it is time to tell the full story: a heady mix of blue-skies thinking; political jockeying with British Rail; over-optimism, sometimes bordering on fantasy; individual personality clashes; and behind-the-scenes rifts between BURCo and the Waverley Association.

The second key dimension of this book is in a largely unpublished selection of 116 photos, most of them taken by Ian Holoran with a Pentax S1A camera in early April and late May 1969. Ian was an activist and office-bearer within the Waverley Association, and undertook a BURCo commission to produce (unpaid) a photographic survey of the route, accompanied – and driven – by his wife-to-be, Christine. Many of Ian's photos – particularly at the closed stations – have a ghostly, *Mary Celeste* quality, portraying a virtually forgotten world of lingering freight traffic from Edinburgh to Hawick (until 25th April), later, the railway which had been abandoned to the track-lifters between Hawick and Longtown on 6th January, and finally, the briefly-surviving freight railway between

Longtown and Carlisle. This will surely be the first and only book on the Waverley Route to deliberately feature not one photograph of its 107-year working life as a passenger railway!

I hope this story, together with the photos, will bring to life an astonishing episode in British railway preservation history. Like me, many readers will doubtless reflect on all the 'what ifs?' and whether a more realistic BURCo rail plan might have delivered a very different kind of railway in the Borders at least 40 years before this neglected region finally got a train service back with the opening of the Borders Railway from Edinburgh to Galashiels and Tweedbank in 2015.

Sources and acknowledgements

By far the main inspiration and source for this story was the late Roy Perkins, whose family connections in Newcastleton and wider Liddesdale provided such solid underpinning of his enthusiastic efforts on behalf of BURCo in 1969-70. I was very lucky to be introduced to Roy by Bruce McCartney during my research for *Waverley Route: the life, death and rebirth of the Borders Railway*, and met him on several occasions, notably on a memorable weekend at his Merseyside home when I was privileged to be taken through his comprehensive BURCo archive.

Bruce, as a Waverley Association (WA) activist and office-bearer (and prior to that a campaigner against closure), also brought many valuable insights, not least into the turbulent relationship between the WA and BURCo – as did Ian Holoran, whose personal archive proved to be invaluable. Ian's photos are a key part of this unique story and I am most grateful for his permission to use a selection of these in the book. My old friend and rail campaigning colleague, Bill Jamieson, was able to identify some of the photo locations which Ian could not recollect, as did Bruce, Iain MacIntosh (in particular) and Matt Stoddon. Bill's careful perusal of a BR track-lifting diagram also allowed me to narrow down to the season / year most of the undated photos taken in 1969-71 by the late Oliver Hudson (courtesy of Rae Montgomery). Rae also provided invaluable help by checking the proofs of the book. Other key sources of photos were Bruce, Bill Roberton, Dougie Squance and Norman Turnbull.

No book about railway history is complete without maps, and once again I am delighted to have bespoke maps hand-drawn by Alan Young – one illustrating the bleak situation of the Waverley Route on 6th January 1969 and the other an enhanced version of one of his original maps for *Waverley Route: the life, death and rebirth of the Borders Railway*, showing details of the rail network between Carlisle and Longtown. In the latter connection, I'm also grateful to Ken Harper and Donald Sills of the Cumbrian Railways Association for clarifying the somewhat complex chronology of briefly surviving freight services and signal

Introduction

box closures in the Carlisle / Longtown / Mossband triangle in 1969-70. Another invaluable information source was the Disused Stations web site: http://www.disused-stations.org.uk/ (which also features maps by Alan Young).

Andrew Boyd was one of the key campaigners against closure, and his insights were an important source for *Waverley Route: the life, death and rebirth of the Borders Railway*. For this book, I am delighted to have been able to reproduce (in the Appendices) Andrew's notes of his unique brake van trip on Trip E10 from Millerhill Yard to Hawick on 24th March 1969 – recording a prosaic contrast to the volume of main-line freight trains just three months earlier, the latter illustrated in the last BR freight working timetable also reproduced in the Appendices.

As well as a variety of private archive sources, I found much useful information in public archives: in particular the National Records of Scotland in Edinburgh and the National Archives in London (Kew). In the latter respect, I am entirely indebted to Bernard Lamb, an 'amateur' archive researcher based in London. In 2010 I was getting tantalisingly close to the final explanation of how and why the Waverley Route closure was approved by Government in 1968, when I had the great good fortune to be introduced to Bernard by Bruce McCartney. It was Bernard's assiduous research at Kew which unearthed key British Rail papers on the BURCo affair (as well as the minutes of the crucial ministerial committee meetings in London which sealed the line's fate). These were the critical last pieces in the jigsaw.

David Spaven
Edinburgh, May 2018

The stone-walled cutting immediately north of Eskbank & Dalkeith station, looking towards Bridge 13 and Millerhill, on 7th April 1969. The photographer, Ian Holoran, had permission from BR – through BURCo – to access BR property. The photo was taken from the 'four foot', but with just one return freight train daily from Millerhill to Hawick – and having photographed it returning to Millerhill earlier that day – he was not taking much of a risk!   *Ian Holoran*

CHAPTER 1

Before the Border Union Railway Company (BURCo)

The history of the Waverley Route, from its origins in the Edinburgh-Hawick railway opened in 1849 – and completion as an Anglo-Scottish main line in 1862 – through to the virtual sealing of its fate in the 1963 Beeching Report, has been written up in some detail by a variety of authors, including: John Thomas and Alan Paterson in *A Regional History of the Railways of Great Britain Volume 6, Scotland: The Lowlands and the Borders* (1984); AJ Mullay in *Rails Across the Border* (1990); and Robert Robotham in *The Waverley Route: The Postwar Years* (1999).

This author takes up the story from 1963 to the present day in *Waverley Route: the battle for the Borders Railway* (third edition published 2017), where he explores the political machinations following the Beeching Report, the protracted demise of the railway, the spirited – but too tardy – campaign against closure, the dramatic events on the last night of operation on 5th / 6th January 1969, then more than two decades in the wilderness, followed by the long campaign for rail re-opening, culminating in the start of train services on the Borders Railway in 2015.

Rather than repeating that history, *Border Union Dream* overwhelmingly concentrates on the little-known and often misunderstood story of the Border Union Railway Company between early 1969 and late 1970. To appreciate some of the key references made in this book, however, we should note a number of individuals who played leading roles in the period immediately before the BURCo saga:

- Richard Marsh MP: the Minister of Transport who in mid-1968 gave his consent to the closure of the entire Waverley Route, rather than retaining the crucial Edinburgh-Hawick section as strongly advocated (in private) by Willie Ross MP, the Secretary of State for Scotland

- David Steel MP: the local Member of Parliament and a key player in the campaign against closure, who threatened to resign his seat to force a by-election focused on the fate of the railway

- The Rev Brydon Maben: Church of Scotland Minister for Newcastleton, a leading light in the campaign against closure from 1966 and a key player in the final disruptive protests on the night of 5th / 6th January 1969 at Newcastleton

- Madge Elliot: Hawick 'housewife', who inspired and led a belated grassroots campaign against closure, and together with David Steel and the Earl of Dalkeith MP delivered an 11,678 signature petition to 10 Downing Street on 18th December 1968.

We should also remember – who can forget? – those remarkable events of 5th / 6th January at Newcastleton station which have gone down in British railway history. A part-planned, part-spontaneous, protest by local people – keenly aware of the serious impact which loss of the railway would have on their access to the wider world – blockaded the level crossing gates at the village station. Led by the Reverend Brydon Maben, the passage of the last train on the line – the overnight sleeper from Edinburgh to London St Pancras – was held up for two hours. Maben was 'arrested' by the police (there remains some conjecture as to whether he was formally arrested or just 'led away'), but David Steel, who was a passenger on the train, eventually persuaded the crowd to disperse if the minister were released and no charges preferred. In due course, the police having released Maben, the level crossing was cleared and the last train continued its journey south, reaching Longtown 117 minutes late and proceeding onwards to Carlisle and St Pancras.

At 2.50am, ten minutes after he had received advice from Newcastleton that the signal box there had closed, the Hawick South signal box register was signed by Gordon Hall, who had swapped shifts with Jimmy Douglas to be the last permanent signalman on duty at Hawick. Twenty-four stations and seven signal boxes had closed, and after 107 years as a through Anglo-Scottish line, the Waverley Route was dead.

On Monday 6th January 1969, Hawick – a town of 16,000 people – suddenly found itself 45 miles from the nearest railhead (Carlisle) and 51 miles from Edinburgh by a very slow and basic bus service, while the 13,000 residents of Gala were left 33 miles by road from the capital. No other towns of their size in Britain were now so distant from the rail network, and the Borders had become the only region of the country with no train services.

BR did not hesitate to demonstrate that their decision was final. As HP White records in *Forgotten Railways* (1986):

Next day [in fact it was on Wednesday 8th January] BR, in the presence of media

Before the Border Union Railway Company (BURCo)

representatives, symbolically lifted a length of rail at Riddings. They had forgotten the Churchillian wisdom: 'In victory, magnanimity'.

The abrupt end of all passenger operations on the Waverley Route and the swift start to track-lifting were not, however, the end of the story.

Four months of vestigial freight from Edinburgh to Hawick

On 21st February 1969, a travelling shunter leads Clayton Type 1-hauled Trip E10 through the closed Galashiels station towards the freight sidings on the Down side.
George Kinghorn (courtesy of Dougie Squance and Bruce McCartney)

Headed by an English Electric Type 3 (aka Class 37), E10 waits to return to Millerhill after shunting Hawick freight depot in late March 1969. Empty oil tanks from Gala – which prior to 6th January would have been attached at St Boswells – are prominent in the train consist, as clarified by A. Boyd's notes in the appendices.
Bruce McCartney

The Millerhill-based 'Secondman' on BR Type 2 (aka Class 25) No. D7608 is perhaps gazing at the almost-abandoned St Boswells signal box (out of shot to the left) during shunting by Trip E10 on 24th March 1969. *Bruce McCartney*

Unconventional hand shunting at St Boswells on 24th March 1969 is assisted by Andrew Boyd (in the gaberdine coat), who had organised the brake van trip on E10 from Millerhill to Hawick that day. Andrew's log of the trip is reproduced in Appendix 2. *Bruce McCartney*

Trip E10 has a modest load returning to Millerhill in early April 1969, passing the site of Darnick Siding, with the Eildon Hills beyond. Today the rail solum has been obliterated over this section by the A6091 Melrose bypass, completed in 1988, but enough space remains to create a single-track railway without major upheaval. *Bruce McCartney*

First of a sequence of four photos illustrating the shunting operations of Trip E10 at Hawick on 4th April 1969. The train from Millerhill has just arrived at Hawick's former Carlisle-bound platform, and the travelling signalman who had joined the train at Gala is climbing down from BR Type 2 (aka Class 25) No. D7607 to work the points enabling the loco to run round the train on the former Edinburgh-bound platform road. *Ian Holoran*

Having running round its train, D7607 pulls out of Hawick station prior to propelling E10 into the freight depot sidings on the Down side. Part of the goods platform in the foreground survives to this day as a walkway leading north from the adjacent leisure centre which occupies the site of the old goods station. *Ian Holoran*

D7607 shunts the coal sidings at Hawick. Contracts with the coal trade for rail deliveries to this depot and Galashiels had forced BR to temporarily retain vestigial freight services after the cessation on 6th January 1969 of all other traffic on the line. *Ian Holoran*

D7607 prepares to return E10 from Hawick to Millerhill, with empty oil tank wagons from Galashiels prominent towards the rear of the train. *Ian Holoran*

First of a sequence of four photos showing the progress of Trip E10 on 7th April 1969. Here the train heads south towards Torwoodlee (between Stow and Galashiels), hauled by English Electric Type 3 (aka Class 37) No. D6847. *Ian Holoran*

D6847 powers E10 up the 1 in 180 gradient east from Melrose on 7th April 1969. The former railway solum here has been obliterated since 1988 by the A6091 Melrose bypass – and threading a future single-track railway through this constrained topography would be difficult, but certainly not insurmountable.
Ian Holoran

D6847 has just burst out of Bowshank Tunnel, crossing the deep-sectioned lattice girder bridge over the Gala Water on the return working of E10 on 7th April 1969. Today's Borders Railway retains double track at this point, one of three 'dynamic loops' on the largely single-track line.
Ian Holoran

A few hundred yards north of Bowshank Tunnel, E10 disappears towards Millerhill on 7th April 1969 with a mixed consist of vans and open wagons, including coal empties from Gala and Hawick.

Ian Holoran

The first of three photos capturing the return leg of the very last Trip E10 on Friday 25th April 1969. Headed by Clayton Type 1 No. D8606, the train ftrom Hawick stands alongside Galashiels box, having dropped off the travelling signalman who had joined the outbound trip here earlier in the day. This was the final revenue-earning train to run on the Scottish section of the Waverley Route until the first passenger train on the re-opened Borders Railway on 6th September 2015.

George Kinghorn (courtesy of Dougie Squance and Bruce McCartney)

The last E10 trip passes Lady Victoria Pit box, and the extensive colliery sidings on the right. Butlerfield Washery is in the distance, to the left of the former Waverley Route.   *Bruce McCartney*

The end of vestigial freight services over the northern section of the Waverley Route: Clayton Type 1 No. D8606 draws the last returning E10 trip into Millerhill Yard on 25th April 1969. A steam-era water tower survives between the two Up loops, with the double track of the former Waverley Route to the left.
Bruce McCartney

National Coal Board No. 3 Andrew Barclay 0-6-0ST hard at work shunting coal wagons at Lady Victoria colliery on 19th May 1969. Coal traffic by rail from the colliery survived only until December 1971, when the remaining truncated section of the Waverley Route was cut back to the Newbattle Coal Preparation Plant, a short distance to the north (on the other side of the former main line) – and this in turn succumbed to complete closure in June 1972. Much of the colliery – closed in 1981 – survives as the Scottish Mining Museum, conveniently served by the modern Newtongrange station.
Norman Turnbull

Edinburgh to Hawick: a *Mary Celeste* railway

The Up side platform and waiting room at Eskbank & Dalkeith on 7th April 1969. The imposing street-level station building above (designed by Thomas Grainger and John Miller) survives to this day. Today's single-track Borders Railway runs mid-way between the two surviving platforms.

Ian Holoran

The signal box at Hardengreen Junction had formerly controlled the north end of the Peebles loop, the junction of which lay immediately below the signalbox. Latterly it had been simply a 'block post' for the main line, one of 14 signal boxes remaining between Carlisle Canal Junction and Millerhill in the final days of the Waverley Route. By the date of this photograph, 6th April 1969, the line here was operating under 'telephone and notice board' arrangements between Millerhill and Lady Victoria Pit.

Ian Holoran

Still operational as the only block post south of Millerhill, Lady Victoria Pit signal box basks in the sunshine on 7th April 1969, overlooked by the distinctive colliery complex. The box would close just three weeks later. *Ian Holoran*

Looking north towards Bridges 23 and 22, between Lady Victoria Pit and Gorebridge, on 6th April 1969. *Ian Holoran*

Prior to closure on 6th January 1969, Gorebridge 'enjoyed' just one train a day to Edinburgh, in contrast to the 33 daily offered by today's Borders Railway. However, the station then benefited from double track and two (partly staggered) platforms, whereas Network Rail and Transport Scotland contrived to provide the modern incarnation with just one track and one platform. *Ian Holoran*

Broken windows were typical signs of recently-closed stations, as in the case of Gorebridge seen here on 6th April 1969, but a general air of neglect would have set in some two years earlier, after the station – together with 10 others on the Waverley Route – was de-staffed in March 1967. From today's perspective, the absence of even a post-and-wire fence between the platform access path and the Down main line is striking. The main station building survives, unoccupied in mid-2018, but with plans for community use. *Ian Holoran*

The photographer was not afraid to take advantage of some precarious vantage points to capture panoramic views of the railway estate, as in this shot from the Down Home signal post at Fountainhall, looking north on 6th April 1969. The former bay platform exchange sidings for the Lauder Light Railway and goods yard are to the right, bounded by the Gala Water. *Ian Holoran*

A close-up of the main station building (dating from 1870) on the Down side at Fountainhall on 6th April 1969. This is one of just three original platform-level buildings which survive beside today's Borders Railway. *Ian Holoran*

The graceful lines of the southern portal of Torwoodlee Tunnel – one of just three on the Waverley Route – are captured in this 7th April 1969 view looking north towards the bridge over the Gala Water, just beyond the northern portal. *Ian Holoran*

The distinctive Bridge 97 – around half a mile north of Galashiels station – is seen looking south on 5th April 1969. Happily, it has survived to provide an important pedestrian right of way across today's Borders Railway. *Ian Holoran*

BR could not be accused of failing to make infrastructure economies in order to reduce the cost of operating the Waverley Route, as exemplified by this shot looking north beside Galashiels station on 5th April 1969. Today's single-platform Gala station – part of a modern public transport interchange – is located close to the alignment of the Up line in the middle distance. *Ian Holoran*

In 1937, in an early signalling modernisation scheme, the London & North Eastern Railway replaced two junction signal boxes, three boxes controlling the Galashiels station layout (making a total of five in just over two miles), and many semaphore signals, with a single 'Galashiels' signal box controlling colour-light signalling and motor-operated points. By 5th April 1969 that box had been closed as a block post for three months, but some of its levers – controlling the nearby freight sidings – were still being operated by the travelling signalman who joined the daily (Monday to Friday) E10 trip freight here from 7th January until 25th April. *Ian Holoran*

The well-proportioned waiting shelter on the island platform at Gala (serving Up trains on the Waverley Route and branch trains to and from Peebles and Selkirk) is redundant on 5th April 1969, yet just three months earlier had been sheltering passengers awaiting two trains daily (Monday to Friday) to Hawick, two to London and three to Carlisle. *Ian Holoran*

Multiple goods offices beside the entrance to Galashiels freight depot, presumably primarily for coal merchants, naturally each had their own coal fire! Doubtless a number of these were unoccupied by the time of this photograph taken on 5th April 1969, looking north west. *Ian Holoran*

Hand-operated cranes from an earlier era survive at Galashiels on 5th April 1969, three weeks before complete closure. In the background are the goods offices (left) and the passenger station building (centre). *Ian Holoran*

Still – just – an operational railway, but only a handful of wagons provide the evidence at Galashiels on 5th April 1969, looking north west. Other than the distant hills and the church in the middle distance, this scene is unrecognisable today, buried under a sea of roads, car parks and retail outlets. The Borders Railway squeezes through a narrow corridor on the far right. *Ian Holoran*

The forlorn former engine shed at Galashiels, seen on 5th April 1969. Opened in the early 20th century, it was a sub-shed of St Margarets in Edinburgh. In April 1962, two months after the complete closure of the Peebles branch, the shed was closed, but was used subsequently for locomotive storage, most famously for the A4 Pacific No. 60026 *Miles Beevor*. *Ian Holoran*

Once more, a signal post has allowed the photographer to capture a panoramic view of the railway – looking north from St Boswells station on 5th April 1969. Much of the Up yard infrastructure remains in situ, while in the distance the oil distribution depot which had been directly served by rail until early January can be glimpsed on the Down side. *Ian Holoran*

Also taken from the signal post, looking south at St Boswells station on 5th April 1969. The main station building is on the Up side behind the goods shed, with all tracks remaining in situ, but on the Down side the bay platform formerly serving the branch to Reston (and, after the 1948 floods severed the railway, Greenlaw) had lost its track some time earlier. The branch was closed to passengers in 1948, and completely in 1965. *Ian Holoran*

St Boswells good shed, its subsidary buildings and the yard's 3-ton crane look in pristine condition in this *Mary Celeste* shot on 5th April 1969 – devoid of goods, people or trains. *Ian Holoran*

St Boswells box, on the Down platform, lies empty on 5th April 1969, as on every weekday between 7th January and 25th April other than during the brief flurry of activity following the late morning arrival of Trip E10 and the travelling signalman from Gala. Formerly known as St Boswells South, the name was shortened following the closure of St Boswells North (and Kelso Junction, to the south) in February 1966. *Ian Holoran*

The imposing St Boswells station frontage (on the Up side) is seen to good effect in this 5th April 1969 shot. The building had formerly incorporated a booking office, waiting room, toilets, refreshment room, post office and the stationmaster's home. Not a trace of this attractive structure is left today.
Ian Holoran

Plain, but attractive, the Down platform waiting shelter at Belses awaits its fate on 4th April 1969. Happily, that fate was was much better than for most other buildings on the Waverley Route, the Disused Stations web site reporting that: 'The station house survives as a private residence . . . The track bed between the platforms has been infilled and grassed but both platform edges are extant. Both platform buildings have been restored and are in good condition' [but note that this is private property]. *Ian Holoran*

Scrambling up a telegraph pole gave the photographer enough height to demonstrate clearly the sheer width of the railway corridor (including the gas works branch on the far right) immediately north of Hawick station on 4th April 1969. *Ian Holoran*

Hawick South signal box (on the Down platform) was re-built in 1913 to improve visibility – and was still providing a commanding view over the railway estate on 4th April 1969. It had become Hawick's sole box when Hawick North closed in June 1965.   *Ian Holoran*

Hawick station had a secondary entrance from Mansfield Road, seen here from the west on 4th April 1969, with the first arch of the viaduct over the River Teviot on the right. The absence of cars (parked or moving) is striking, but the lack of road congestion en route to Edinburgh did not help former rail travellers, who now faced a two and a half hour bus journey, compared to one and a half hours or less on the train. *Ian Holoran*

The graceful viaduct over the River Teviot is seen from the east on 4th April 1969. The bridge and the entire railway station complex were razed to the ground in 1975, with a leisure centre later being built on the site of the old goods station. *Ian Holoran*

CHAPTER 2

The rise and fall of BURCo

On the evening of 8th December 1968 a Londoner with family connections to Liddesdale dropped into the local Wellington Arms pub in Woolwich, to celebrate his birthday with a near-neighbour. Roy Perkins' mother was from Newcastleton and he retained extensive family connections in the area, including no fewer than five Uncle Archies scattered across Liddesdale! The conversation between Perkins and Martin Symms ("who had rather less than no interest in railways") soon turned to the imminent closure of the railway through Roy's spiritual home village. From this unlikely beginning was hatched an initial plot, reminiscent of an Ealing Comedy, to prevent operation of the replacement Hawick-Newcastleton bus service by reversing an HGV into the parapets of the Sandholm Bridge north of Newcastleton.

Together with Perkins' work colleague at the industrial giant Michelin, John Turner, the group set off by car the next weekend to reconnoitre the situation at Newcastleton, but once back in London this dangerous 'direct action' idea soon evolved into a breathtaking plan to preserve the entire Waverley Route as a going concern. Following an introduction – by a common acquaintance in the vintage car business – to the TV producer Bob Symes-Schutzmann, then working on *Tomorrow's World*, and a known enthusiast for rail preservation, an urgent letter was delivered by hand to David Steel at the House of Commons. Steel came out of the Chamber to meet Perkins (who had worked for Steel's 1965 by-election campaign, and was employed in market research) and Symms (who had travel and real estate interests), and a productive dialogue began. At Perkins's suggestion, harking back to the line's genesis in the mid-19th century, the name chosen for the company was the Border Union Railway Company (BURCo).

The first actual reference to the nascent BURCo in Roy Perkins' personal archive is a copy of a 17th January 1969 letter from Ian Holoran (who subsequently undertook the comprehensive photographic survey of the line, and was the first Secretary of the voluntary support group, the Waverley Association) to Mr G Hinchcliffe of Flying Scotsman Enterprises, extolling the potential for steam operations in the Borders once BR's planned ban on main-line steam began in 1971. Holoran's personal archive reveals that, just two days later, Hinchcliffe responded to the effect that:

> whilst we are very interested in your project and can see endless possibilities in

it for us we are too heavily committed with British Railways to tie ourselves with any scheme of this kind…In spite of this Mr Pegler and myself feel that there is much in the idea which might in the future be of mutual benefit. I am therefore asking that I be allowed to know far more about the scheme than I usually feel inclined to know. I would also like the opportunity of meeting some of the business men involved and if possible sit in on a board meeting as an observer…Until I know more I am not prepared to give any support of any kind from this organisation.

There is no archive evidence that the discussion went any further, but the first response to the BURCo concept filed in Perkins' archive is a 30th January letter from Brian Hollingsworth of Buckinghamshire, who had experience of main-line steam operations. Hollingsworth offered perceptive and cautionary advice:

I'm still gasping about yr. amazing project…I sincerely wish that I could agree with you that it is 'on'. As regards the serious operation of the route for commercial purposes, it is unthinkable that either the Govt. or BR would give you the opportunity to prove that you could do it and they couldn't. Personally I don't think the sort of changes that a private group might make would have a significant effect on the losses. Remember Lord Ailsa & the I.O.M. [an abortive attempt to revive the full Isle of Man narrow-gauge network as a commercial concern].

He noted that none of the various established steam operations round the country had annual revenues greater than around £70,000 – and BURCo were projecting £150-200,000 – and supplied a graph plotting estimated costs (over and above volunteer assistance) against length of line, which suggested that "a 20-mile stretch is as great as could be viable in the long-term." Hollingsworth's view was that the best chance of success would be for BURCo to concentrate on Newcastleton to Hawick, as he did not consider "that the clientele likely to be discouraged by the absence of a rail passenger connection would be significant in relation to those who would be attracted by the more spectacular part of the line." This was perceptive advice – and such a scheme could also have developed timber traffic utilising the 15 additional track miles from Newcastleton to Longtown (and onwards by BR metals), with the prospect of longer-term re-opening for tourist trains from Carlisle and excursions originating elsewhere on the BR network. But BURCo had grander plans…

The initial phase of this ambitious project concluded one weekend in January, dominated by an amusing railway incident which, with hindsight, could have been tragic. Advised that some track had already been lifted at Riccarton Junction, the group drove north overnight from London, calling at Newcastleton to pick up Perkins's cousin, son of a now-redundant signalman at Newcastleton. Riccarton was of course notoriously difficult to reach by road, so the car headed for Whitrope Siding, two miles to the north of the isolated junction, but with no particular plan in mind. Perkins's cousin spotted a pair of old bogie wheels lying beside the track, and these were promptly re-united with the railway and kicked off in the direction of Riccarton. The wheels had little trouble moving off down the 1 in 80 gradient, and if they turned up at Newcastleton, 10 miles down the line, this would prove that the track was still extant! Realisation quickly dawned, however, that children could be playing on the track and that the falling gradient continued to just beyond the level crossing gates at Newcastleton…

In near-panic, Perkins and company hurtled down the road, and placed some stones on the track at Steele Road, backed up by a discarded rail jack. Time passed, and the group had just about given up (assuming that the track had indeed been severed at Riccarton), when the wheels came whistling round the bend from Arnton Fell at 25-30 mph, brushed the stones aside, hit the wheel jack, flew five feet in the air and crashed, safely, on to the sleepers. The would-be railway preservationists adjourned to the Grapes Hotel for a short celebration then drove back to London, somewhat wiser about the power of the railway and the inescapable fact of gravity!

A strange half-life

The entire Waverley Route had closed to passengers on 6th January 1969, but contracts with the coal trade forced BR to maintain a daily freight train – Trip E10 – from Millerhill Yard to Galashiels, St Boswells and Hawick, and return, through to 25th April.

The existing signalling system – designed for a relatively busy, double-track, main line – was no longer required, but both Up and Down tracks remained in use, using a simple 'Telephone and Notice Board' operational control arrangement. The signal boxes at Hardengreen, Heriot and Fountainhall were closed as 'block posts', with – as noted by the BR internal instructions – 'all points disconnected out of use pending removal . . . and all signals removed', the only exceptions to the latter being the retention of Distant signals at Heriot and Fountainhall to protect the level crossings (with the gates being operated by trainmen).

Galashiels, St Boswells and Hawick South signal boxes were closed as block posts, but retained as 'ground frames' controlling the crossovers and connections to remaining goods sidings. At St Boswells, the Up sidings for 'general merchandise' traffic were retained, but the Down sidings were disconnected, removing access for tank wagons to the rail-linked regional oil depot. BR was able to retain the traffic until 25th April by detaching the oil wagons at Galashiels, with piped discharge to road tankers for the final road leg to St Boswells.

South of Millerhill, only Lady Victoria Pit box (just south of Newtongrange) remained as a block post, and the signalling system was downgraded to Telephone and Notice Board working between Millerhill and Lady Victoria Pit, and between Lady Victoria and Hawick, permitting just one train to operate at any one time on the latter 42 mile, 1,078 yard section, which was reported in the railway press at the time as being the longest 'block section' on British Rail. A travelling signalman joined E10 at Galashiels each weekday to operate levers at the remaining ground frames. At all the former boxes – not just those re-designated as ground frames – a telephone 'connected to the Lady Victoria Pit / Hawick circuit' was provided for use by trainmen.

As well as oil wagons to Gala, coal was delivered to Gala and Hawick, plus a variety of general merchandise traffics to (and from) all three 'full load' depots. According to the Hawick South signal box register (part of a surviving private archive), the first freight of the Waverley Route's strange half-life arrived at Hawick on Tuesday 7th January at 13.50 on the Up (to London) line, and returned to Millerhill at 15.00 on the Down (from London) line. The absence of a service on Monday 6th January presumably reflects the need to use that day for a squad of men to disconnect most of the points, to remove almost all signals and to install the revised telephone links and new notice boards, prior to the commencement of a highly-rationalised operation the next day.

The Hawick South register had also recorded the fate of the southern section of the Waverley Route, as far as the BR Scottish Region / London Midland Region boundary. The signal boxes had been closed at Shankend, Riccarton, Newcastleton and Kershopefoot and all signalling equipment had been put out of use, pending removal, and:

> With effect from 1100 on 6th January 1969 complete possession of the Up and Down lines has been taken between 53 M.P. [mile post] at Hawick to 84M 1170 yards below Riddings by the Engineer. J Hope PW Inspector, James McBain Tfc Inspector.

The daily freight to Hawick had relatively modest volumes of business to handle, so a 'Clayton' Type 1 (aka Class 17) of just 900 horse power, was all that was usually needed, even with the stiff climb at 1 in 70 over Falahill Summit. However, this was a notoriously unreliable class of loco, and Millerhill traction maintenance depot would often roster other loco types for the E10 turn, including English Electric Type 3s (aka Class 37s), of 1,750 horse power, which had been a mainstay of Anglo-Scottish freight working over the Waverley Route in the last few years of its life. Their now humble local task contrasted with previous Millerhill-Kingmoor front-line duties, typically non-stop through the Borders, as illustrated by the last BR freight working timetable reproduced in the Appendices.

The lingering freight-only railway could readily turn a blind eye to practices which might have been frowned on while the Waverley Route was still a secondary main line. Ralph Coleman, who – as described in the author's *Waverley Route: the battle for the Borders Railway* (Third Edition 2017) – had been probably the youngest official objector to closure back in 1966, recollected in 2012 how as an enthusiastic 12-year old he kept pestering the local Gala parcels clerk (who had not been made redundant on 6th January 1969) to speak to the E10 trip driver and ask if he could have a footplate ride to Hawick and back:

> I was usually given the 'green light', and had a number of memorable trips, including one occasion when the usual low-powered Clayton Type 1 diesel was replaced by a 2,750 horse power Brush Type 4 [aka Class 47, another class regularly seen on the Waverley Route in its last years] which allowed some pretty fine running between St Boswells and Hawick.

The Hawick South signal box register (presumably signed by E10's travelling signalman from Gala) intermittently records details of freight and track recovery train arrivals and departures until a final detailed entry on 4th March 1969. Prior to that, the register shows that on Wednesday 8th January the second E10 of the freight-only era arrived in Hawick at 14.30 (returning to Millerhill at 15.12), hauled by 'Birmingham' Type 2 (aka Class 26) No. D5310 – which happily now survives in preservation on the Llangollen Railway in north east Wales.

Other survivors of Waverley Route operation include a remarkable six from the last four days of full Anglo-Scottish service (2nd-5th January) – as detailed in *Waverley Route: the battle for the Borders Railway* – including Birmingham Type 2 No. D5340 (aka class 26), which worked passenger trains between Edinburgh and Carlisle on the 2nd, 3rd and 4th, including the author's last journey, on the 10.20 ex-Riccarton Junction to Edinburgh on the 2nd. Appropriately, this loco is now in preservation with the Waverley Route Heritage Centre at Whitrope.

Back on the freight-only railway to Hawick, Andrew Boyd (who had been a key campaigner against closure) was at the time also a regular organiser of 'brake van trips' for Edinburgh University Railway Society, and arranged a special trip by brake van on E10 on Monday 24th March 1969, for himself and two of his campaigning colleagues, Eric Glendinning and Bruce McCartney. As was customary, the fare charged was the equivalent of a First Class ticket, in this case 26 shillings for the single journey for each passenger (the equivalent of around £15 today) – a veritable bargain for such an historic journey! Andrew reckons they were therefore the last fare-paying rail passengers to Hawick.

Andrew wrote up notes of the journey – reproduced in full in the Appendices – which was to be his last on the Waverley Route. Yet another loco type – BR Type 2 No. D7608 (aka Class 25 of 1,250 horse power) – was deployed on this occasion, reaching speeds of 45-50mph on both the downhill gradient from Falahill Summit and over the relatively straight and easily-graded section between St Boswells and Hawick. At various stages of the journey, the train carried coal, oil, sawn timber and potato wagons – all traffics which probably would have survived the next decade or more on the truncated railway, had Richard Marsh made the right decision in mid-1968.

Despite occasional locomotive reminders of past glories, however, the Waverley Route was now just an operational shadow of its former self – but, behind the scenes, its potential strategic future was the subject of feverish activity.

BURCo develops a business plan

Perkins, Symms and Symes-Schutzmann were getting to work with a vengeance on formulating their business plan, networking in every possible direction with contacts in the railway, business, financial and public relations worlds. So committed was Perkins, a qualified economist, that he resigned from his market research job with Michelin, moved to Newcastleton, and worked full-time on the project for nearly a year. In part he was able to fund this 'sabbatical' from the proceeds of his small business (restoring vintage cars) which he had kept going through university and beyond.

One of Perkins' first tasks was to produce a Draft Report on the proposed North British Railway Company (NBR), which was intended to be the operating company, leasing the line's assets from the holding company, BURCo. This report, which is part of the Perkins' personal archive, contains many more financial build-up figures to support the bottom-line conclusions than the Feasibility Study which was eventually publicly launched in late August. Like the feasibility study, however, it makes big claims for how the railway would regenerate the Borders tourist economy without a great deal of robust analysis to support this conclusion. Nevertheless, the range of potential markets identified and the detailed breakdown of operating expenses projected indicate that this was very much a serious venture.

The rise and fall of BURCo

Interestingly, the basic cost projections in the Draft Report were built up from BR Annual Report data to derive figures on the various cost categories per route mile / per running track mile etc – so BURCo were making no extravagant across-the-board claims about private sector cost-cutting to transform BR inefficiencies. Instead, Perkins – and it was he rather than Symes-Schutzmann or Symms who undertook most of the analysis and number-crunching – identified specific areas where cost elements could be cut and where revenue could be increased, in some cases (such as operation of all regular trains with diesel multiple units) where both could be achieved by a single initiative. On the cost side, taking advantage of the greater flexibility of working practices which private sector operation would allow, all stations other than Hawick would be unstaffed, and – although neither the Draft Report nor the later Feasibility Study mentioned this – quotations were provided by a control systems company for on-train ticket-issuing machines.

The Draft Report indicated that as double track was to be retained, no intermediate signalling would be required to maintain a 90-minute frequency service north of Hawick (thereby reducing signalling costs, albeit leaving a heavy track cost), but by the time the Feasibility Study was published BURCo was advocating track singling, and by implication one of two crossing loops which would have necessitated signalling of some sort. Selective use of volunteer enthusiast labour, for example for supplementary track work, was also a key component of the cost reduction strategy.

On the revenue side, the combination of a regular-interval service, lower fares (of which more later) and improved marketing would stimulate substantial revenue growth for the core service, while an entirely new market for steam-hauled tourist services was at the heart of the business plan. The Draft Report acknowledged that due to the hiatus since closure a certain amount of traffic would be permanently lost, but calculated that, "78.3% of existing traffic level at closure must be recaptured in order that the railway breaks even in its early years."

Most of these strands of innovative thinking made a lot of sense in themselves, but the core challenge for a railway nearly 100 miles long – as opposed to the single figure lengths of most of the 'preserved' railways in Britain – was to demonstrate that it was realistic to project bottom-line costs and revenues so dramatically transformed that a heavily loss-making (and state-subsidised) line could be turned quickly into a private enterprise operation which would earn a conventional profit. While very different approaches to the market and to costs – compared to those of BR – were being projected by BURCo, there was an enormous gulf between the latter's aim of profitable operation and the figures quoted by BR in the period leading up to the Ministerial consent to closure: an annual saving from complete closure of £536,000 and a grant requirement of £700,000 per annum to keep the whole line open in perpetuity.

To meet this challenge, the NBR Draft Report was circulated in mid-February (confidentially, until an evident embargo date of 15th March 1969) to potential investors and/or opinion leaders, including as we shall see some key individuals of whom a majority would in due course become 'associates' of BURCo. The 25th February response from James Kyle, County Clerk of Roxburgh, did not provide much encouragement at this early stage of the project, but neither did it close the door:

> I found the report most interesting but I cannot help feeling that it is over-optimistic... I feel sure that my Council will be interested in your projected development and you will no doubt let me know when I would be free to raise the matter with them.

Around this time, the well-known London-based solicitor Mark Bonham-Carter (a personal friend of Symms) was instructed to set up a limited liability company. By the time of Roy Perkins' 27th February letter to Brydon Maben, the former was able to advise that "we should very shortly be a corporate body" and that "B.R. have been approached, contact having been made with both the B.R.B. [in a 26th February letter] and the Scottish Railway Board, and the reaction, I am very relieved to say has so far been extremely favourable." Perkins indicated that "talks start next week", but there were also cryptic references to difficulties in terms of reactions to the Draft Report's attribution of costs to different elements of the rail service, and to a delay in the planned survey of potential rail users – the first of a noticeable number of references to BURCo delays and/or mislaid correspondence during the course of 1969.

Wider support for BURCo

Perkins had also approached another near-neighbour, John Grant, who promptly suggested setting up an enthusiast support group for the company – and the Waverley Association (WA) was soon established, with Grant as the Secretary. Grant was an experienced businessman (and a future director of Bovis Homes, as well as working for the preserved Bluebell and Kent & East Sussex Railways), and more should have been made of his skills, but as Perkins recollected in 2010:

> There was a fundamental clash of personalities with Bob Symes-Schutzmann. Both had very strong personalities, and for some reason Bob wanted to appear to be the businessman, when in fact he was a TV producer and railway enthusiast.

The rise and fall of BURCo

There was also an evident wish on Symes-Schutzmann's part to keep the Waverley Association at arm's length, in order to avoid BURCo being labelled as preservationists.

Ian Holoran, the Secretary of the WA, reflected in 2011, "it is true that John Grant and Bob Symes-Schutzmann had the same strong personalities which clashed, but I think the main reason for this was that John disagreed with many of Bob's proposals."

In addition to the original encouragement to set up an enthusiast support group, it was planned to establish the North British Railway Company (NBRC) as a holding company to keep liabilities separate, and during the course of 1969 an impressive list of planned board directors for the NBRC was lined up, including Michael Lycett (insurance broker and Lloyds' member), Hugh McMichael (an Edinburgh accountant), J Mathieson (Chairman of Scottish TUC and NUR), Lord Melgund and William Strang-Steel (both Borders landowners), Noel Penny (former MD of Rover Gas Turbine), Colonel Simmons (Curator of Railway Exhibits at the Science Museum), and Lesley Stewart (MD of Stewarts Spinners).

In practice, the company was never set up, but six of the above (all bar Mathieson and Simmons) – plus two other individuals – were to become 'associates' of BURCo who played the closing cards on behalf of this ambitious but ultimately unsuccessful project in late 1969 and early 1970. There seems to have been little or no contact between the majority of these associates and the directors until a 'summit meeting' of 18th October 1969 (of which more later), with Roy Perkins recollecting that his only regular meetings were with Lesley Stewart. With hindsight it looks to have been a major strategic failing that this impressive body of business and financial expertise did not have more involvement with the directors, in particular Perkins, to assist in the development of a business case.

BR presses on with track-lifting

While the replacement bus service haphazardly bedded in along the twisting A7 road between Edinburgh, the Borders and Carlisle, the dismantling of sections of the railway proceeded, within the constraints of a Ministerial requirement for the route formation (ie the land but not the track) north of Hawick to remain *in situ* for two years. The author has examined, within a private archive, a BR diagram (nearly 15 feet long!) of track age, type and disposal plans covering the entire Waverley Route within Scotland, showing planned selective lifting by BR of rail on the 'Up' (to London) line for re-use elsewhere on the network, after the symbolic breaching of 820 yards at Riddings on 8th January. The base information appears to date from immediately post passenger closure, but the diagram was continually updated through to almost the last track-lifting activity late in 1972.

Lifting took place at a variety of locations along the Up line of the Hawick-Riddings section between January and March, both tracks of which were now under engineering rather than operational control. The oldest rails lifted in early 1969 had been laid in 1952, and the newest dated from as recently as 1965; stretches of concrete sleepers were also recovered. Allan McLean, who worked for BR in Glasgow in the early 1970s recollected in 2010 that a section of track for the upgrading of the West Coast Main Line near Beattock was taken from the Waverley Route near Whitrope – the BR records point to this being 730 yards of flat-bottomed track immediately to the north of the tunnel which had been laid as recently as 1962. Other than the Whitrope section and another short stretch to the south of Shankend station, all the early track recovery took place south of Riccarton Junction. In total, half a mile of bullhead panels (ie intact sections of track comprising rails and sleepers), nearly 7 miles of flat-bottomed track panels, and $2^2/_3$ miles of bullhead rails were recovered for use elsewhere. The Down line, however, remained completely intact.

This period of early track-lifting is also recorded by entries for 'ballast' trains (a catch-all description for engineering traffic, including track-lifting trains) in the Hawick signal box register, from January through to Tuesday 4th March, when Clayton diesel No. D8607 arrived 'light engine' from the north at 09.40, having entered the section (presumably at Lady Victoria) at 08.15. Sister loco No. D8606 then left light engine in the Down direction back towards Millerhill at 09.42. On the Down page for the same day is a handwritten note "D8607 ballast from Engineers Rd. [as the line south of Hawick under engineers' control was described] at 14.35" and that is the last detailed entry until the final entry in November 1969 (other than the daily trip freight E10 from Millerhill, through to its last run on Friday 25th April) – a period of track-lifting inactivity which reflected the ongoing negotiations between BR and BURCo, as we shall see.

BURCo's public launch

The BURCo plan was publicly launched at a press conference held at the prestigious North British Hotel in Edinburgh on Saturday 15th March, chaired by David Steel. The group faced a barrage of questions from the media, and soon received generous local and national press, television and radio coverage. A great deal of public interest was immediately generated by the prospect that the last major railway to be closed in Britain could become (to quote David Henshaw in *The Great Railway Conspiracy* (1994)) "the test-bed for a new and radical idea: a privately-owned and fully commercial trunk line." On 20th March, along with extensive front-page coverage of the rail plan, the *Southern Reporter* included an editorial, which commented:

> At a press conference in Edinburgh on Saturday the three directors exuded confidence and enthusiasm. But it takes more than these qualities, valuable though they are, to make a success of such an undertaking…Much, very much more, requires to be known about the venture before one could give it a yea or nay, but certainly it should not be dismissed nonchalantly as mere 'pie in the sky'. It is at least worthy of full and fair consideration.

While this high profile was being maintained by the directors, the Waverley Association (WA) was determinedly chasing potential steam locomotives for the railway. On 27th March 1969 Garth Dawson & Co of Accrington billed the WA for that day's inspection of locos at Lostock Hall Motive Power Depot, advising the presence of Class 5s 44894 ("no shed plate"), 45017 ("10A") and 45388 ("10D").

The WA also seems to have had the more prosaic task of acting as an administrative back-up to Bob Symes-Schutzmann, with two letters in the space of one week in April conveying tickets and travel arrangements for his journeys to Scotland. On a wider front, while the growth of WA membership was a reflection of the way BURCo had captured the imagination of many railway enthusiasts and rail supporters, how was the nascent railway preservation movement reacting to this potentially mammoth interloper? Norris Forrest of Aberdeen had written to Ian Holoran on 9th March, advising that the BURCo scheme had been mentioned the previous day at a meeting of preservation societies in Scotland, and:

> the SRPS [Scottish Railway Preservation Society] just laughed at it. Most people are not taking it seriously and until the directors can produce some money I doubt if much money will flow from Scotland. I think their best bet is to concentrate on the Borders and the various Councils. Railway enthusiasts will just not bite. If they can raise £60,000 and obtain suitable negotiations with BR, then some notice might be taken.

Interestingly, as recollected by Roy Perkins in 2011, BURCo received "tens of thousands of pounds" of unsolicited donations, much of it from Borders expatriates in North America. The directors decided to treat these funds with extreme caution – being concerned about possible fraud accusations – and none of it was touched, and indeed in the end all was returned to the donors.

While it was reasonable to conclude that most or all of this money was sent to help directly with the purchase of the railway, the reality was that the purchase could never happen without a robust business case, and this in turn – as we shall see later – would depend on a thorough and independent feasibility study. With hindsight, these donations might crucially have been used for such a study, to identify what fundable business case, if any, lay at the heart of the BURCo proposition.

Back in the British rail preservation world, the Secretary of the SRPS wrote to Holoran only two weeks after reports of its scepticism about BURCo – and perhaps significantly, in terms of BURCo's credibility, just a few days after the latter's public launch – advising that it was pressing ahead with its plan to reopen the Aviemore to Boat of Garten line as a preserved railway – but that no final agreement with BR had yet been signed, and should the Aviemore project not come off it might have to look for an alternative location in Central Scotland, in which case, "it might be to the mutual advantage of both our organisations for us to have a site on or near your line of route. We would probably prefer to be near Edinburgh, say at Lady Victoria."

This raises another tantalising 'what if?' about the Waverley Route. The SRPS eventually pulled out of the Aviemore scheme (leaving the successor Strathspey Railway to turn it into reality) and in due course made a great success of their base at the Bo'ness and Kinneil Railway. But were they tempted by the Lady Victoria option once BR pulled out in 1972? A preserved railway at this Newtongrange location would eventually have found itself beside the popular Scottish Mining Museum, and if it had remained linked to BR at Millerhill, then one of the future major breaches of the railway solum – by the Edinburgh City Bypass – might never have happened. This in turn would have made the eventual re-opening of the railway through to Gala and Tweedbank on the one hand significantly cheaper, but on the other hand it is anyone's guess how the SRPS might have reacted to a request for their heritage railway to move aside for 'the real thing'! Perhaps it could have bargained for the entire operation to be relocated at government expense to the Selkirk branch or the former Light Railway from Fountainhall to Lauder…

Widening ambition

A further measure of the scale of BURCo's early ambition was indicated in terms of the route infrastructure which came within the company's orbit of interest. On 26th March 1969, prompted by "local Trade Unions", Berwickshire County Council wrote to Symes-Schutzmann about the imminent lifting of track between Tweedmouth, Kelso and St Boswells, advising that it considered this and the potential re-opening of the railway was a matter for the 'Eastern Border Development Association' and flagging up pressures on local authority expenditure and borrowing consents from government. The interest was short-lived – in an 11th April letter to Martin Symms, BRB in London advised that "Mr. Symes-Schutzmann telephoned me this morning to say that your interest in the purchase of the St. Boswells-Tweedmouth line is now at an end." It might seem that BURCo were indulging in flights of fantasy by contemplating an even bigger scale of rail operation, but in fairness it was Kelso Town Council who had originally urged the company to consider this extension – and wider public relations' considerations possibly played a part in BURCo's initial response.

The directors of BURCo (Symes-Schutzmann, Perkins and Symms) followed the public launch with a series of meetings with potential investors, and – according to Perkins, recollecting events in 2010 – initial confidential backing came from the merchant bank, Noble Grossart, and the Bank of Scotland. Perkins recalled that Minister of Transport Richard Marsh tried very hard to identify which banks were talking to BURCo, presumably in order to put pressure on them not to back rail re-opening, which would have been highly embarrassing for the Government.

On 30th March, Ernest Tait of the Border Economic Planning Group wrote to BURCo requesting an outline of its financial plans and the proposed timetable, for discussion at the next Group meeting. Perkins and Symes-Schutzmann had a hectic programme in Hawick on 9th April, meeting four textile companies in the morning, then sessions with the Waverley Line Action Group (belatedly set up in September 1968 to fight closure, and comprising local authorities, business and other interests and MPs) and the Chamber of Commerce in the afternoon, followed by the Chamber dinner in the evening. A note also advised that, "Mr. Simpson of B.R. Hawick Station, could meet the directors at the Chamber Offices on the afternoon of Thursday, 10th April" – whether this meant that the erstwhile Area Manager was still based in Hawick, with just one freight train a day to manage, is not clear!

Minutes of the Action Group meeting record Symes-Schutzmann expressing the hope that "businessmen and the public in the Borders would stand to benefit from the re-opening of the Line and that accordingly they would support the project by taking up Shares in the Company." In a sign that BURCo really had caught the local imagination, the Minutes also record that Madge Elliott and two others "reported that they were aware that employees in local factories had been enquiring how they could save up towards purchasing Shares and how they should go about applying to purchase Shares." Symes-Schutzmann told the meeting that "BR had been most co-operative to date".

Roy Perkins' archive reveals that BR agreed a three-month embargo on track-lifting from May 1969, but as the evidence points to this activity having already ceased in early March, the 'embargo' may have been as much a reflection of BR having secured sufficient serviceable track to meet its immediate needs elsewhere on the network as it was a sign of good faith with BURCo. To assess the overall state of the infrastructure, BURCo commissioned detailed engineering and photographic surveys of the route, and both of these were undertaken during April and May 1969 – the former by RC 'Reg' Harvey (the company's engineering consultant, formerly of Randall, Palmer & Tritton), and the latter by Ian and Christine Holoran.

The end of freight

During the period of freight-only operation – in January 1969 according to the Waverley Association's June 1970 newsletter – Hawick Town Council asked BR to run a special train to a rugby international at Murrayfield stadium in Edinburgh. BR's reply stated that the signalling system was not up to passenger standard, and in 2011 Bruce McCartney recalled his 'wry amusement' that BR managed to run rail tours in 1970 and 1971 from Millerhill to Lady Victoria Pit, where exactly the same signalling system was in place. One can only assume that BR in 1969 was much more concerned about the potentially dangerous politics of running a passenger train to Hawick than the revenue which this would generate.

The last freight train from Millerhill Yard to Hawick ran on Friday 25th April, hauled by the same type of locomotive – the distinctive Clayton with its elevated central cab – which, as the Hawick 'pilot' loco sent ahead of the passenger service to check out the integrity of the line, had played a key part in the dramatic events of 5th/6th January at Hawick and Newcastleton. The Claytons were one of the least successful of the BR Modernisation Plan diesels – and all were withdrawn by 1971 – but will always be associated with the Waverley Route because of their role in these events and their frequent use (double-headed) on through freight trains. In 2017, Andrew Boyd recollected that with "Bruce [McCartney] on his motor-bike and myself holding on for dear life behind" they went down the A7 road to look for the last northbound train, spotting it near Bowland, with D8608 hauling some 34 wagons. At the level crossing gates (closed to the railway) at Fountainhall, they encountered – travelling with the guard – a BR management trainee, David Masterton, whom Andrew knew through SRPS. Andrew comments:

> According to my notes, David Masterton told me there were about 20 wagons left at Galashiels; St Boswells had been cleared; and there were 15 left at Hawick. Once their loads had been discharged, the empty wagons that were left would have to be cleared by a special ad hoc trip, possibly some time during the following week. However my notes are silent as to when such a train ran.

The rise and fall of BURCo

On 27th April 1969, the ground frames at Hawick South, St Boswells and Gala – and the remaining block post at Lady Victoria Pit box – were shut, and the last revenue-earning traffic had been carried over the 43 route miles from Hawick to Lady Victoria. A road-served BR parcels and sundries operation was, however, retained at Galashiels for a number of years.

As local MP, David Steel was continuing to back BURCo – although in correspondence with the author in 2010 he commented that, "I clutched at any straw, but really they were away with the fairies" – and Hansard for 28th April 1969 records that he, "asked the Minister of Transport what assistance his Department is giving to the Border Union Railway Company in its proposal to provide a public railway service on the Waverley route", to which [Richard] Marsh's reply was that, "Following an exchange of correspondence, officials of my Department had a general and helpful discussion with representatives of the Border Union Railway Company on Friday, 25th April." Who attended and what was discussed is not known.

The BR response develops

Freight was one of the issues flagged up in the first detailed letter from the BRB Estates Manager to BURCo on 12th June, in anticipation of a BRB / BURCo meeting in Melbury House, London, on 20th June: "There ought to be no difficulty in accepting freight trains in to Millerhill and Kingmoor, but we shall need to have more information about the methods you propose for operating freight traffic." The initial tone of the letter was also positive about a key issue – "there would appear to be no insuperable difficulty in accommodating your services over the Board's lines in to [Edinburgh Waverley and Carlisle Citadel stations]" – but there were quite a few significant stings in the tail, including:

> At Waverley Station, the Board have development plans which will make it impossible for your services to run in to the east end. It should, nevertheless, be possible to accommodate you in the suburban platforms, though precise timings cannot be guaranteed, and adjustments might be necessary…At Carlisle, the Port Carlisle branch which gave access from the N.B. line into the station was isolated some time ago. This would require to be reconnected, involving the crossing of the up and down goods and up and down main lines in order to reach the bay platform on the up side. This work, including resignalling, would have to be carried out at your company's cost…Under no circumstances whatsoever can the Board permit the working of steam locomotives over their lines…Your company's services must at all times take priority behind the Board's services, whether the latter are running late or otherwise…The Board will not be prepared to offer co-operation in respect of through bookings nor in respect of excessing.

Interestingly, the BRB letter also flags up its intention to abandon the Longtown-Mossband Junction freight spur and retain Longtown-Carlisle in the event of BURCo operating over the latter section of the Waverley Route – necessitating additional BURCo running powers, but also "some reduction to the [outright sale] figure of £1.3m. which we will work out." The letter also referred to the need to discuss the "A74 road scheme" – the planned Carlisle bypass, which, crucially, would breach the route of the railway and therefore require an expensive (£200,000) new bridge. In due course BURCo were asked to pay for this, and eventually agreed to do so subject to certain conditions – the implication is that (a) the route at either end of the bridge would remain BR's, and (b) this arrangement would allow BR to save some money by closing Mossband Junction (which had only opened in 1963) as part of the West Coast Main Line (WCML) upgrade. This seems like convoluted thinking on the part of BR, who surely must have realised that the cost of the new bridge would help to kill the BURCo project

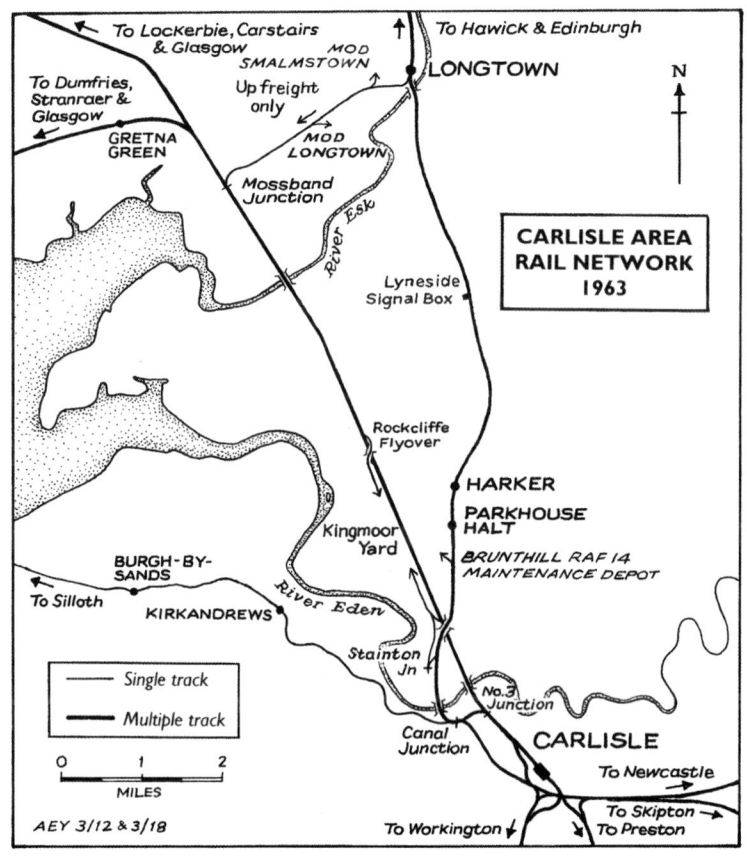

Alan Young

In practice, it was the former Waverley Route section south from Longtown to the connection for the Brunthill RAF depot which closed (in August 1970), with BR installing a WCML crossover at Mossband Junction to enable Down as well as Up trains serving the Longtown military sidings to take this route. The latter outcome would of course have been perfect for BURCo, avoiding the cost of building the new A74 bridge and purchasing the Longtown-Carlisle section. However there is no direct archive evidence that such an offer was made while BR and BURCo were in discussion throughout 1969 – despite BR having planned in 1967 for just such a scenario, should the Minister refuse consent to Waverley Route closure (as explained in the author's *Waverley Route: the battle for the Borders Railway*).

It is certainly an odd unexplained episode, further complicated by a quotation (within a February 1991 letter by Frank Spaven, the author's father) from the Scottish Railway Development Association's December 1969 newsletter to the effect that, "[BURCo's] plans have been modified to use the Longtown-Gretna railway, thus saving £150,000 in costs of a road bridge on the Carlisle bypass on the direct rail approach." Ironically an internal BR memo of less than a year later (6th April 1970) implies that the A74 bridge was at best a red herring and at worst a deliberate attempt to scupper the BURCo project:

> To avoid bridging the [Carlisle-Longtown] line north of Brunthill at a cost of about £170,000 the M.O.D. have confirmed that they will defray the Boards' costs in adapting the Mossband/Longtown Line for bi-directional working to enable the Longtown Freight traffic to be worked from Carlisle over that line.

BURCo's extensive shopping list

BURCo had a big shopping list for rolling stock to operate its all-year and tourist services, the Feasibility Study (which was not published until August 1969) referring to "two diesel locomotives, seven diesel railcars and six steam locomotives, in addition to 22 passenger coaches, four bogie parcel vans and sundry goods and service vehicles." According to an article in *Railway World* magazine later in 1969, in addition to the core rolling stock, Symes-Schutzmann – it seems to have been his personal idea alone – had plans to "purchase a complete Austrian train", the former Emperor's no less! In his defence, however, Symes-Schutzmann pointed out to the author in 2011 that these coaches – intended to be used in connection with filming rights (of which more later) – were otherwise heading for the scrapheap.

BURCo's extensive shopping list did not faze the BRB's Chief Engineer (Traction & Rolling Stock) who on 31st July wrote encouragingly to Symes-Schutzmann about the potential availability of seven DMUs stored at Carlisle, and advised that he had made contact with a potential BURCo Chief Engineer, of whom he had "not the least hesitation in saying there will be no more suitable man in Great Britain." Another *Railway World* article (in December 1990) reported that, "An LMR P/way engineer, John Fleetwood-Shaw, was designate General Manager."

According to *Railway World*, BURCo associate Noel Penny and BR engineers had discussions about converting traditional DMUs to gas turbine drive: "With axle-hung turbines of new design and drive cut-out to allow for coasting, the units could have been economical with excellent acceleration and introduced the Sprinter concept a generation earlier." However, the required technology was, at the time, unproven in such a use and presumably would have been very expensive. The diesel engines in the DMUs earmarked for BURCo (2-car 'Derby Lightweight' units) were in any case generally reliable if maintained on a regular basis, and would have been adequate for the proposed services for a good number of years. Similar engines in other classes lasted much longer, although the deteriorating state of the units' bodies would have been more of a concern. The same article referred to the planned introduction of innovative non-British operating practices, based on knowledge of Austrian and Swiss systems:

> [Symes-Schutzmann] approached Maj Rose of the Railway Inspectorate with a proposal to use radio signalling, and got approval in principle. Another planned feature was a simple 25kV overhead electrification, tramway-style, from Carlisle to Riccarton. This would link up with the electrified WCML (then still incomplete) to allow BR electric locomotives to work through to Riccarton at 25mph, to collect timber trains.

While radio signalling and electrification would certainly have been innovative, it is questionable whether the cost of the latter in particular could have been justified for no more than one or two freight trains daily. But new ideas were a key characteristic of the whole BURCo vision – from (for example) flexible working practices, through turnstile access to stations, a franchised on-train catering service, and airline seats, to "the modelling of locally manufactured garments at Hawick and Galashiels stations during peak traffic periods". An improbable international dimension briefly emerged, with the WA advising members in a 20th May update that:

> Fairmont Railway Motors Incorporated of Fairmont, Minnesota, U.S.A. has requested testing facilities on the Waverley Route for their Hi-Rail equipment, which converts ordinary road vehicles to vehicles suitable for rail operation . . . If the present bid to reopen the line is successful, the Border Union Railway could be the first company in Europe to use the Hi-rail equipment.

The rise and fall of BURCo

The projected cost of the core passenger fleet (including spares) was £55,000, but the earlier NBR Draft Feasibility Report only mentions diesel-multiple units and states that these would be "bought at scrap value and withdrawn when in need of major repair." Quite how they were to be replaced is unclear. A number of redundant BR vehicles were earmarked for purchase, including the Derby-built diesel multiple units, and in an internal memo of 2nd January 1970 the BRB Supplies Manager cryptically notes that:

> I still have on hand at Carlisle 16 condemned vehicles earmarked for B.U.R.C. These can be disposed of almost immediately and perhaps you will tell me whether or not you consider any action can be taken as the longer they lie at Carlisle the more they will deteriorate.

Research by Bernard Lamb – who unearthed key BR documents in the National Archives at Kew – suggests that these units had formerly worked on the Keswick and closed Silloth branches, and were of a type which had all been withdrawn by late 1969. As Lamb noted in 2011, BR were not in the habit of withdrawing stock that had plenty of life left in it. There must have been a good reason to withdraw the Derby units in 1969 rather than refurbish them, partly explained by the state of the alloy body parts and the weakness of the cab design, and this raises the question as to the practicality and cost-effectiveness of BURCo being able to undertake this work.

BURCo tries to stack up the figures – but sees the first clouds on the horizon

In defence of BURCo's part-professionalism, the company was clearly keen to take advantage of established rail experience in developing its business plan. It soon approached Gerry Fiennes, who, in his role as General Manager of BR Eastern Region, had done much to over-turn the conventional wisdom on rural railways, demonstrating one of the key omissions of the Beeching Report by showing that 'Paytrains' and 'Basic Railways' could cut costs dramatically on loss-making lines, while still retaining and even increasing patronage. Fiennes was sacked by BR following controversial comments about frequent management re-organisations in his seminal book, *I tried to run a railway* (1967).

Fiennes met Roy Perkins in London in early June 1969 – partly with a view to producing a magazine article endorsing the scheme. In his 13th June letter to Perkins, Fiennes commented that he "enjoyed our discussion enormously" and asked for gaps in the traffic and financial data to be filled in so that he would be "able to judge whether I can do the article." The annotated data sheets accompanying his letter identified a BURCo projected staffing of 70-76, compared to BR's 345, and revenue of "£427,000 plus" compared to expenditure of £367,000. The critical chunks of revenue were £180,000 for passenger traffic (compared to BR's £107,000); £70,000 for summer tourist traffic; £80,000 for parcels traffic (compared to BR's £38,000); and up to £50,000 for timber traffic. As we shall see, Fiennes continued to correspond with BURCo until late October, but the magazine article was never published.

The envisaged drastic reduction in staffing was clearly critical to the economics of the plan – only part of this reflected the use of volunteers, much more being attributable to securing cost efficiencies such as destaffing stations and introducing more flexible working practices. BURCo had discussions with the NUR (and, according to Symes-Schutzmann at the Campaign for Borders Rail 2009 AGM, secured an 'in principle' offer of a £150,000 investment stake from the union), who accepted the offer of sole negotiating rights for staff. According to the *Railway World* of December 1990:

> the NUR's Sid Weighell, after initial caution, was quite positive about the venture. He accepted that to survive, the line would need fewer staff than formerly. The proposal of paying the national average wage with no overtime but a profit-sharing system was acceptable, as was a no-strikes clause and worker participation in management. An operating rule book was drafted with NUR agreement.

The article in *Railway World* magazine in November 1969 reported that employees would be paid an above-average wage "commensurate with their considerable responsibility", and that it was intended to introduce a profit-sharing and management participation scheme, which had "already led to a vast number of applications from serving as well as past BR employees from all over the country to work for the BUR." How vast that demand from potential employees really was we shall probably never know, but 'outside' volunteer help was certainly crucial to the BURCo project development work – and regrettably the partly personality-based schism between BURCo and the Waverley Association (WA) prevented the former taking full advantage of the latter. The three directors of BURCo had taken on a monumental workload – and it showed. The theme of delays in getting responses from BURCo, and of 'time running out', for example, are recurring features of the archive.

One highly regarded volunteer was the Reverend Brydon Maben, who had been such a central figure in the campaign against closure and in the events of 5th / 6th January at Newcastleton. Maben had concerns about the state of the railway infrastructure, particularly after the residual freight service to Hawick ceased on 28th April. On 16th June, Maben wrote to Martin Symms at BURCo, reporting on the same day's "six-hour check-up on the rail position" at various locations north of Hawick, his general conclusion being that, "I mustn't swear, but BR Scotland are a lot of B------S!" The report was as follows:

- St Boswells – "The bell mechanism and 'block' have been removed from the signal box – 'recently' according to an ex-B.R. man at Galashiels. The station and yard have suffered little vandalism."

- Galashiels – "Some siding track has been removed, but this was 8-9 weeks ago. Electric cables were severed 3 weeks ago by a contractor. No serious problem, I am told. (Valuable maple tree removed!)

- Stow – "All in order. No vandalism."

- Fountainhall – "B.R. removed the 'block' and bell mechanism, levers, and signal arms 3 weeks ago. Box unlocked. Level crossing gear removed."

- Heriot – "B.R. completely gutted the signal box only 3 weeks ago. Levers etc are lying in a heap outside the box. The man in the adjacent cottage assures me that this took place no more than 3 weeks ago. The squad had orders to cut down the signal columns, but these orders were cancelled. Box unlocked."

In June 1969 the WA invited the Earl of Dalkeith MP – who had accompanied David Steel and Madge Elliot on the previous December's delegation of Waverley Route campaigners to 10 Downing Street – to become its President. He declined, "after most careful thought", principally on the grounds that, "I am not prepared to indicate support or opposition to the project until I have seen in writing and had time to study a detailed prospectus" – and he would have a long wait.

However, around this time, an (undated) mid-1969 newsletter of the Waverley Association reported that, "agreement in principle was reached on running over British Railways metals at Carlisle, also between Lady Victoria and Edinburgh Waverley". Also contemporaneously, a draft contract was circulating within BR referring to sale of the railway between Longtown "and the junction with the Board's East Coast Main Line railway…in the County of Midlothian" – almost as if the Board had forgotten about the existence of Millerhill Yard!

In practice, behind the scenes, the bad news was becoming as frequent as the good. Just 10 days after Gerry Fiennes had written to Roy Perkins querying gaps in BURCo's traffic and financial data, the Hawick Manager of The Royal Bank of

Scotland (RBS), AM Turnbull, brought perhaps the first intimation that raising capital for purchase of the railway and associated rolling stock was not going to be as straightforward as the directors had hoped or claimed. Turnbull had met Symes-Schutzmann (and Symms) at a meeting with the South of Scotland Chamber of Commerce in Hawick on 10th June, at which the latter had asked what block financial support could be arranged under the auspices of a merchant bank in Scotland. This seems fairly late in the day for such a key question, but the RBS Manager had undertaken to write to see if the bank's own merchant bank, National Commercial & Glyns, would be interested. What kind of financial submission or business plan had accompanied this request is not clear – and it is striking that Roy Perkins, who had undertaken virtually all the financial analysis, played no part in this initiative – but the 23rd June answer was short and to the point:

> Having examined the submissions my Head Office have now replied that the Bank regretfully cannot help and that there would be no point in having a meeting with them to discuss the matter in depth. I need not go into the terms of the reply further but there is no encouragement.

This was the bluntest of dismissals, and together with Fiennes' queries, must have been the first clear indications that BURCo's grand plan (as opposed to a more modest project on just part of the Waverley Route) was – or was seen to be – of doubtful viability. The pressure was building on BURCo, and on 1st July a letter written on behalf of the BRB Estates Manager, CL Smith, to Symes-Schutzmann advised that:

> At the end of the [20th June] meeting you told us that you expected to be able to let the Ministry of Transport have answers to their questions [from Lt. Col. McNaughton of the Railway Inspectorate] by the end of last month and I shall be glad if you will please let me know if the questionnaire has been returned to them. You will appreciate I am sure that time is running out.

In a striking juxtaposition to the emerging weakness of the fundamentals of the project, in a 7th July letter to a supporter, WA Secretary Ian Holoran, commented:

> Both the Border Union directors and ourselves are very keen to see just what Bob Schutzmann's colour scheme looks like. The very mention of grey conjures up visions of sombre battleships, but Bob assures us that, teamed with silver and black, it is very smart.

The rise and fall of BURCo

BURCo unveils the train timetable

Undeterred by clouds on the horizon, in mid-July BURCo unveiled its provisional timetable – "calculated in collaboration with the BRB" according to the WA's August 1969 newsletter – comprising 10 trains a day between Edinburgh and Hawick, and four daily from Hawick to Carlisle (with an extra return service for millworkers travelling from Newcastleton to Hawick). Compared to BR's seven and six respectively, this seemed a sensible re-allocation of resources to match realistic markets for rail. A standard timing of 1 hour 25 minutes from Hawick to Edinburgh was envisaged, with intermediate stops at St Boswells, Melrose, Gala, Stow and Gorebridge, as well as at new stations at Hawick Burnfoot, Tweedbank, Galashiels Langlee and Galashiels North. BR's last DMU timings (on Sundays) were 1 hour 19 minutes, with just three intermediate stops, so BURCo was evidently projecting significantly faster sectional timings, presumably based in part on the singled track being slewed at many locations to ease the speed constraints of the old Waverley Route's "sinuous succession of curves", as memorably described by AJ Mullay in *Rails Across the Border*.

Utilising insider advice from the rail industry, elasticity of demand for Borders rail travel had been explored in detail (echoing a suggestion of Professor Wolfe in 1967, following his Edinburgh University report on the Waverley Route for the Scottish Office), and a strategy of lower simpler fares was modelled – a BURCo return from Gala to Edinburgh (valid for six months) would cost 9s, compared to BR's 11s 6d day return and 18s ordinary return. As Perkins recollected in 2011:

> Hawick and Gala in 1969 were relatively independent and self-sufficient communities with little 'need' for external communication. This was the background against which my market research and modelling were conducted. In these conditions you would expect high levels of demand elasticity. We were not disappointed.

Perkins also reflected, based on researches during post-BURCo work with Merseyside Transport, that a number of BR managers were clearly aware of demand elasticity issues, and that some traffic was being charged more than it could bear, but they were generally not allowed to implement the appropriate pricing policies until the advent of nationwide 'Saver' tickets some years later.

According to the *Scotsman* of 14th July, "proposed rates for freight will be disclosed when the company's feasibility report is completed in about two weeks" – a target that would be overshot by a month. However before BURCo could take over and operate the railway, they would require to obtain the necessary statutory powers. For this purpose they intended to apply to the Minister of Transport for one or more Light Railway Orders (LRO) under the Light Railways Act of 1896. This legislation was repealed in later times. Perkins was quoted as commenting that, "Any objections to the Orders could lead to a public inquiry, which would delay matters. We are still hoping, however, to be in operation before the winter." While 'light railways' are typically thought of as having a 25 mph speed limit, Andrew Boyd (in his working career a solicitor in private practice, as well as a rail enthusiast) points out:

> There is no statutory definition of a light railway. Equally there is no maximum speed limit laid down in the 1896 Light Railways Act, but frequently a 25 mph limit was imposed, given the nature of the particular railway. The reason for BURCo wishing to proceed in this way was to take advantage of provisions in the Light Railways Act whereby an LRO could be applied for to authorise the working of an existing railway as a light railway and the relevant powers transferred to another company. Otherwise they would have had to obtain a private Act of Parliament to transfer the existing powers held by BRB to themselves.

Despite such outward signs of progress, however, behind the scenes the BRB Estates Manager's office was expressing more concerns, a letter of 29th July stating:

> I have had no acknowledgements or replies to my recent letters and am concerned, firstly that you have not yet let us have copies of the revised prospectus which you told us at the meeting on 20th June you would be producing. Will you please let me hear from you without further delay.

Nevertheless, on 28th July, no less an authority than the office of the Chairman & General Manager of BR London Midland Region (RLE Lawrence) had written to Symes-Schutzmann advising the names of four "possible retired railway officers who could help you in the mechanical and electrical engineering field." On 5th August BRB was still co-operating: a letter to Symes-Schutzmann enclosed a line diagram for the Waverley Route within Scottish Region, and promising similar for the LMR section. But familiar concerns were also to the fore, asking BURCo to "let me know as quickly as possible exactly what [Scottish Region] track you wish to purchase so that a firm quotation can be prepared. The absence of any word from you recently is giving cause for concern."

The Feasibility Study is launched

BURCo's Feasibility Study, published by the public relations company David Block Associates (but largely written by Perkins and Symes-Schutzmann), was published on 27th August, significantly later than forecast. The next day, the *Scottish Daily Express*, under the headline "We'll lower fares, say Border men", reported that the capital necessary to get the project under way would be £1.5m (of which £750,000 would be for purchase of the line), with the company putting up £600,000 and the rest found by the formation of a public company and the issuing of shares. The key role of tourism was emphasised, with BURCo having "provided for the purchase and development of at least two hotels, and will expand – either by buying or establishing participation in a chain of hotels and restaurants throughout the Borders." This was a big story, and Roy Perkins was interviewed by Border TV on 27th August. On the 29th, with the headline "'Full steam ahead' for Border rail plan" the *Hawick News* reported that:

> The Waverley route will be in operation once more within six months and will make a profit of up to £150,000 in its first year. This is the confident forecast by the Border Union Railway Company who are about to buy the line from British Railways.

A core daily service with diesel units over a single track would operate every 90 minutes between Hawick and Edinburgh, and five times daily south of Hawick. A second track was to be maintained between Hawick and Newcastleton, for steam-hauled tourist trains from Galashiels to Newcastleton, appealing to car-based tourists in Edinburgh and the Lake District. This second track was also seen as offering potential for international filming contracts – since this stretch of line had superlative scenery but, as *Railway World* magazine put it in 1990, "without too many features to label it with any national character". The Feasibility Study picked up on the missed opportunities of the 1950s:

> It is a practicable proposition to re-open the line as, in the main, a single track railway. In fact B.R. might have taken some [sic] course fifteen years ago when the southern end could have been modified in the Carlisle area to advantage and the route operated more economically but with the traffic capacity needed.

BURCo's plans were certainly highly ambitious, including the planned new stations. Using only volunteers, including (as revealed in Roy Perkins' archive) a prodigious effort of encouragement and co-ordination by Madge Elliott, the company – according to a 21st July WA update – had secured "8,000 returns of the Passengers Users Survey" of potential rail users in the Borders and beyond, utilising relatively sophisticated interviewing methodology to avoid over-estimation of demand. Overall a 10% sample was achieved; ironically this evidently dropped to 5% in Melrose, which proved to be the town most enthusiastic about the return of the railway. Together with revenues from rental of redundant station buildings, income from a planned railway museum at Melrose and filming rights, the all-year passenger, tourist passenger, freight and parcels markets were to generate a gross revenue of "£485-£578,000 plus".

BURCo had also decided that its headquarters would be at lonely Riccarton Junction, whose only vehicular access was by a Forestry Commission road. Bruce McCartney vividly recalls one member of the SRPS describing that decision as "the zenith of absurdity".

In hindsight, with reported predictions of 8%-10% returns on investment, "rising to possibly 23 per cent later", the financial prognosis can be viewed as hopelessly over-optimistic. BURCo had a vision which effectively aimed to use the railway as a catalyst to restructure the tourist sector of the Borders economy. This was an extremely bold aspiration, and surely depended on optimum outcomes in all the key building blocks of the project – external funding, purchase price from BR, running powers over BR metals, passenger and freight traffic growth, etc.

The BURCo Feasibility Study – while still fascinating to peruse nearly 50 years on – reads in hindsight more like a scoping or pre-feasibility study, with not enough of the market quantification and financial analysis that a genuine business plan would have delivered to convince potential investors. It was long on optimistic commentary on the dramatic difference BURCo would make to the fortunes of the railway, but rather short on robust justification for concluding that such a transformation would be commercially viable.

A week before the Feasibility Study was published, the Waverley Association had advised Symes-Schutzmann that: "Membership stands at 101. Enquiries are still coming steadily" – but the study report was soon to cause problems, as the Waverley Association Management Committee subsequently highlighted (on 20th October) in a terse letter of complaint to the BURCo directors which clearly indicates that the relationship between the two organisations was finally breaking down:

> Directly we received the first copies [of the Feasibility Study] we were appalled to see the number of spelling errors etc in the book and we were almost at the position of saying that the report would not go out [to the enthusiast market] under the W.A. banner due to this fact.

The Association did in fact send out the first batch of 100 copies, and were assured by BURCo that a new edition was going to the printers, but this proved to be a running sore for several months – and encapsulated the way in which a dream (or to the sceptics, a fantasy) was beginning to crumble. While presentational errors might have been less problematic if the basic underlying analysis was demonstrably robust and underpinned by transparently solid quantification, this report did not provide that crucial dimension. Roy Perkins had argued that selected elements of the financial build-up detail in the NBR Draft Report would strengthen the Feasibility Study, but Symes-Schutzmann was worried that some of the figures "would alienate BR" – this was ironic, given that the core cost data had been based on BR's own figures – so the basis for many of the bottom-line financial conclusions in the study remained unclear to the reader. This was clearly a strategic error, and BURCo would soon be alienating BR in a much more profound, indeed terminal, way.

It can be argued that Symes-Schutzmann's greater age and experience (in the media rather than business) and his larger-than-life personality led – in the words of one of the other key protagonists – to "too much time and effort spent on bluster and public relations in the mid months of 1969 rather than on refining the work started with the NBR Draft Feasibility Report which could have yielded some usable hard figures." Roy Perkins reflected in 2011 that:

> As a 23 year old economist and market research analyst I was of an analytic and forensic disposition whereas Bob Symes-Schutzmann was quite the opposite and tended to speak first without consultation – a creature of a type I had never before encountered, though I was to later. As a result I was happiest being the 'backroom boy', whereas Symes-Schutzmann was every inch the presenter. In consequence I finished up being put in a position of having to justify jaw-dropping remarks on the basis of inadequate analysis. Had I been allowed to continue with the NBR Draft Report I still believe that when the 'crunch' came in October 1969 its production would have bought us much needed time.

The wider reaction to BURCo

After the immediate flurry of overwhelmingly positive press coverage, media doubts about the viability of the project began to emerge, a generally balanced report by John Cribbin in the *Edinburgh Evening News* of 9th September commenting:

> The difficulties of running a railroad – as British Rail found out long ago – are that the costs are staggeringly high and that much more than just bright ideas and individual enthusiasm are needed to make a project pay. Already the people in major Borders centres who used to pay more than £100,000 a year in fares and

freight for their use of the line have begun to drift away and are losing the 'railway habit'.

The reporter had interviewed Ernest Tait, Chairman of the Borders Consultative Group which had fought so hard to save the railway, but Tait "states baldly that he doesn't believe this new plan is going to work" without Government subsidy. He nevertheless wished the project well and "[would] encourage all support for them, short of making any large personal investment in the scheme." As BURCo had been making strong pleas for Borderers to invest in the railway, this was not a welcome verdict. Meanwhile, the Scottish Railway Development Association, which had argued strongly against closure north of Hawick, noted cryptically in its September 1969 newsletter that "explicit statement has not been made regarding the sources of the £1.75 million needed to secure re-opening."

Gerry Fiennes was also trying to reach conclusions on the BURCo plan, and in his 9th September letter to Symes-Schutzmann he highlighted some of the key differences between the figures provided by Roy Perkins in June and those shown in the Feasibility Study, including the latter's £210-250,000 for annual passenger traffic (compared to the former's £180,000), and in the case of tourist traffic, £150-200,000 and £70,000 respectively. Overall, Fiennes noted, "Between the two sets of [revenue and expenditure] figures there is a swing favourable to your project of £180/280000 in the first year." The letter gently hinted at some (understandable) impatience:

> I had hoped, before putting a shoulder to your wheel by doing an article or articles for the national Press and by giving you an introduction to possible sources of the loan which you need, to have had a reply to my letter of 13th June to Perkins.

Referring back to the need to fill gaps in the original financial data, Fiennes noted that the Feasibility Study in part did this, "but it does not answer some of the second round of questions, which have to be answered satisfactorily if I am to cheer you on rather than the reverse." Fiennes queried the scope for devising an all-year timetable sufficiently attractive to generate "a 300 per cent increase in the number of people travelling compared with last year of B.R.'s operation", and wondered whether the experience of the preserved Dart Valley and Ffestiniog railways (in established tourist areas) really supported BURCo's tourist traffic projections, concluding that:

> Naturally these are the harder questions which occur to me. So take no offence, where none intended. Nor do I take offence if you think it too much trouble to convince a doubting Thomas.

Perkins nevertheless did eventually reply on behalf of BURCo in a lengthy (undated) hand-written letter which sought to answer all Fiennes' queries. Among the points covered were the key role of Edinburgh as a major established tourist centre (and the location of the 1970 Commonwealth Games) supplying potential custom for BURCo's tourist trains; the proximity of major roads such as the A7 and M6 to bring in car-borne custom for the steam railway; and BURCo's unique capability to accept excursion trains from the BR network and to operate main-line steam. In his reply of 30th October, Fiennes noted that Perkins had advised that he was "drawing up a document in a form more acceptable to accountants than the feasibility study. I will wait for a look at that before commenting in detail". That, however, is the last communication from Fiennes in the archive.

Plans for freight

While Fiennes' primary interest was in passenger traffic, BURCo had also set out big plans for freight in the Feasibility Study. A key market would be tapping into the massive Forestry Commission plantations of Kielder, Kershope and Newcastleton (which had been strategically planted during the inter-war and post-war years), initially to be served by a Newcastleton railhead, and forests west and south of a planned Galashiels railhead. Harvesting had just begun in the southern forests, and the transport requirement was forecast to grow at a rate of 6-7% pa over the next 5-10 years, causing potentially major problems on inadequate local roads.

On 23rd June 1969, the Forestry Commission Conservator for North East England advised BURCo that in Kielder Forest alone production would rise from 45,000 tons in 1970 to 75,000 tons in 1974 – with the production expected to be destined for the key rail target mills in Ellesmere Port and Workington rising from an estimated total of 33,000 tons in 1970 to 42,000 tons in 1974

In joint talks it was concluded that two big timber trains a week (rising to one train a day by the mid-1970s) could be justified from a reinstated Kielder spur of the old Border Counties Railway from Riccarton to Hexham. In co-operation with Powell-Duffryn an innovative containerisation system for timber was demonstrated at Longtown freight depot on 3rd November 1969, allegedly offering substantial cost-savings over conventional road-to-rail handling methods. However, a photo on page 112 shows an unusual end-loading/unloading technique which if used as shown in normal operations would have involved intensive rail shunting operations for every wagon, unlike the simpler lateral movement which has been the standard method of road-rail transfer of containers from the 1960s until the present day. The WA's November newsletter reported that the trial had been viewed by the Forestry

Commission, BR, the press and other local interests. Its comment that, "A certain amount of shunting rail wagons will be necessary at the railhead [envisaged to be at Newcastleton, as BR had contemplated in a study in late 1968] because of end loading", was something of an understatement.

However, BURCo's plans for other freight traffic were, in general, characterised by both innovation and realism about what the railway could do cost-effectively in the early 1970s – and they could hardly be blamed for not foreseeing that the ongoing overall loss of freight from rail to road in Britain would continue for another two decades. Domestic coal was seen as a declining, but temporarily worthwhile traffic, while livestock was rightly dismissed as more suited to road haulage, as was rail's fast-declining textile traffic – other than a premium long-distance service to the key London market.

Papers in the personal archive of ex-BR manager Rae Montgomery (now held as part of the North British Railway Study Group archive at the National Records of Scotland in Edinburgh) indicate that in the last period of BR operation a weekly winter train of 18-30 wagons of sugar beet pulp (for animal feed) operated between Bardney in Lincolnshire and Hawick. BURCo saw this – and road salt – as part of its planned freight portfolio, and discussions began with Royal Mail on tendering for letter and parcel mail, which were then still core traffics on the rail network (and of course had been carried on BR's Waverley Route trains until the final days).

The most imaginative of BURCo's freight concepts was for the development of 'Pick-A-Back' (aka 'piggyback') traffic carrying conventional road trailers on low-platform rail wagons. This system, which simplified road-rail transfer, was being pioneered in mainland Europe (and continues to hold a niche share of the intermodal rail market on the continent to this day). BURCo's feasibility study commented that: "the use of these vehicles will be invaluable because of the company's proximity to the M6 on one hand and Leith Docks on the other" (for flows identified between Leith and Liverpool Docks). With a fleet of low-platform piggyback wagons (costing £10,000 each, at 1969 prices), BURCo saw the potential – as in other markets – for the Waverley Route to act as a test-bed for the wider British railway network.

While piggyback has never established a permanent presence in this country (partly due to the very restrictive 'loading gauge' through tunnels and bridges in Britain), its potential long fascinated proponents of rail freight development, with the Government agency Scottish Enterprise investing in a prototype wagon as late as the 1990s. However, in the context of the 1960s' Waverley Route, it is hard to avoid the conclusion that this was a highly speculative and unproven market.

Other than in the case of timber and perhaps Royal Mail, it can reasonably be concluded – in hindsight – that the majority of their freight targets would either never have materialised, or if they had come to rail, would before long have declined or disappeared as part of the widespread loss of wagonload traffic to a road haulage industry whose efficiencies were increasing in leaps and bounds on the back of heavier and faster lorries and the expanding motorway and trunk road network. The Borders was largely not rail freight territory, a point which had been brought out clearly six years earlier in the Beeching Report's Map 4 of Freight Traffic Station Tonnage, which showed that the Waverley Route had no locations in the highest tonnage category (over 25,000 tons pa) and just three in the intermediate category of 5-25,000 tons (Gala, St Boswells and Hawick). Every other station fell into the lowest category of less than 5,000 tons, and all of these had lost their freight facilities by 1968.

The beginning of the end for BURCo

Following the late August launch of the Feasibility Study, routine correspondence continued between BR and BURCo for several months. On 18th September, the BRB Estates Manager wrote to Symes-Schutzmann about BURCo's track requirements:

> On 5th August I wrote to Mr. Symms to send him full details of the whole of the permanent way in the Scottish Region part of the line. I have since been given to understand by Mr. Duncan, our Sales Controller, that the information sent to Mr. Symms has been mislaid and that Mr. Duncan produced copies, including the London Midland Region part of the line and sent the whole lot to Mr. Harvey [BURCo's engineering consultant]. Nothing further has been heard and we thus still do not know what permanent way your Company will wish to seek to acquire, with the result that we can take no action about disposal of the remainder. You will, I am sure, recall that our original undertaking was to defer lifting the track for three months from last May and you will understand that I am under some pressure because there are assets in the shape of the track lying idle with a value in excess of £1m.

There was a very practical reason for the delay – around this time Martin Symms had actually dropped out of the picture; his travel business had got into trouble and he was forced to concentrate his energies on making a living. This left all the BURCo workload on just two individuals, but in practice overwhelmingly on Roy Perkins who was now working full-time for the company. As late as 10th October the BR Estate Surveyor in Glasgow – in response to a request from Hawick Burgh Council to take down a boundary fence to accommodate a footpath which would be entirely on Council land – wrote to BURCo asking "if you will consider the application and advise me whether you are agreeable to my granting permission to carry out the work involved"!

Border Union Dream

There was still enough evidence to suggest that BRB were genuinely willing to negotiate, but behind the scenes Gordon Stewart, BR Scottish Region General Manager, was far from happy. In his letter of 3rd October to Roy Hammond, the BRB's Chief Secretary, Stewart's view was crystal clear:

> I am getting really concerned at the work, which I am quite sure will be abortive, which is having to be done because of the Border Union Railway. We are now, apparently in the process of drawing up a Light Railway Order etc. and meantime no effort has been made by anyone to find out just how the promoters intend to finance their scheme…Mr Symms[sic]-Schutzmann and his partners are having a merry game playing at railways and we are paying the piper!...I am sorry to be persistent about this but I really think these people are just playing a game with us and it is time somebody asked them very decidedly about money.

Stewart wanted an immediate demand for payment of interest on deteriorating assets, and was unhappy with the growing belief that running powers had been conceded into Edinburgh Waverley, noting that while Scottish Region could physically accommodate trains "at certain times" this could only be done if *the BRB* was prepared to grant running powers. The bombshell for BURCo then came in the transcript of a letter from HM Herbert, the BRB Deputy Secretary, (and former Divisional Manager at Inverness) as read out over the phone to Symes-Schutzmann on the morning of 6th October. The "terms on which the Board are prepared to proceed" included the following:

- to sell the freehold of the line between Lady Victoria and Longtown, together with the permanent way and fixed equipment, for "between £745,000 and £960,000" [of which £75,000 would be for land and buildings], subject to contract and the grant of a Light Railway Order

- running powers into Edinburgh and Carlisle at an estimated charge of £125,000 annually, plus "the Company to pay the actual cost, currently estimated at £85,000, of capital works at Carlisle, Longtown and Edinburgh, necessary to permit the exercise of running powers"

- the Company to pay the Board, "before negotiations proceed", £10,000 towards the Board's administrative costs; "such sum to be retained by the Board if the Company are unable to complete the transaction" – an item evidently not costed in the Feasibility study

- a deposit of £250,00 to be paid into the bank on 1st December in the joint names of the Board and the Company

- as from 1st December, the Company to pay interest at the rate of 10% pa on a minimum of £495,000, "being the balance of the value of the permanent way materials which the Board would otherwise have recovered and disposed of. This interest to be retained by the Board in any event."

The letter concluded by advising that "the Board would like to have evidence of your ability to meet the full capital demand as soon as possible" and "acceptance of the basic terms by not later than the 1st December." The read-out text of this letter, together with a virtually identical version sent to BURCo on 4th November, was a massive setback. Not only were significant additional capital (up to £250,000 more) and revenue (up to £50,000 pa more) costs being quoted, but also the directors faced a critical early deadline and associated demands for delivery of funds, some of which would not be returnable if the scheme did not proceed. One may speculate why the letter was only read out initially and was not sent to BURCo for another four weeks – did BR hope that this would stimulate early action by BURCo in terms of demonstrating their financial backing and general backing, so that BR could then have the comfort that it could continue with confidence to negotiate along the lines of the earlier sale offer?

While Symes-Schutzmann was mulling over this shock news, an article based on an interview he had given to a personal friend, RA Barnes, was in the printing presses of *Railway World* magazine. As we shall see, the new information this brought to the public domain – before the Waverley Association had had the chance to inform its members – was to be another strand in the unravelling of the relationship between the support group and BURCo. While Symes-Schutzmann must have given the interview some weeks before the fateful 6th October call from BRB, the article nevertheless paints a much more encouraging picture than the reality of the project's development justified:

> Progress has been so swift and successful that as I write this article the board of the operating company, to be known as the North British Railway Company Limited, is being constructed with a view to running the first passenger trains probably during the early part of 1970…A large part of the [£750,000 purchase price] sum has been promised, and the company feels confident that when stock is issued on the open market they will have no trouble raising the remainder.

In practice, as this was being written, there was still no robust analysis to demonstrate the commercial viability of the project, no private sector funding had been committed, and BR management was becoming increasingly exasperated at the lack of supporting evidence to justify continuing negotiations. The blows were now raining down hard on BURCo, and BR's serious doubts about the company's ability to raise the necessary finance were vindicated (without BR knowing it) by a response on 15th October 1969 from the Edinburgh merchant bankers, Noble Grossart Ltd, to Symes-Schutzmann's submission of the Feasibility Study for their consideration. Nobel Grossart may have given initial confidential backing to BURCo earlier in the year, but their response to the sorely inadequate Feasibility Study was unsurprisingly negative. Unfortunately, only the first page of their letter survives in the Perkins' archive, but its message is clear:

> We have concluded that it would not be an attractive investment from our point of view for three reasons. Firstly, we think that you have underestimated the capital requirements and the operating expenses under several heads. Secondly, we do not share your belief that the anticipated traffic on the line will increase to any significant extent. Even if there were to be a material increase in the population of the Border area, we do not think that there will be any necessary connection between that growth and the use which would be made of the railway. Thirdly, we do not think that the venture has any real prospects of growth in the next few years. In our opinion this is not a venture which is starting at a modest level and growing but a static or declining situation which at best can be revived by enthusiasm and made to operate at a low rate of profitability.

Once again, Roy Perkins had had no involvement in an important initiative, and a potential funder had nothing more to go on than a largely qualitative report, with no explanation of how the bottom-line cost and revenue figures had been derived. Noble Grossart doubtless knew little about railways – including the experience of reprieved lines (albeit rather different from the Waverley Route, by then closed for nine months) often turning round their fortunes through operating efficiencies, improved services and better marketing – but the message was clear. The financial market did not believe the BURCo prognosis on costs, revenue and growth – the business plan, such as it was, did not convince.

The BURCo 'associates' take over

Although potential directors of the planned operating company for the project (the North British Railway Company) had been lined up for many months, the penultimate identified letter written on behalf of the Border Union

Railway project (by Lord Melgund to the press on 5th February 1970) states that, "The Directors of B.U.R.C. and their associates met *for the first time* [author's italics] at a meeting called by Mr. Symes-Schutzmann and held at Crewe on Saturday 18 October 1969." It seems extraordinary that it took so long for such a meeting to take place, presumably prompted by BRB's drastic telephone ultimatum of 6th October to Symes-Schutzmann.

For some months there had clearly been a wealth of business and financial experience potentially available to assist and support the directors, and one cannot doubt that some or all of them would have been keen to work with Roy Perkins to strengthen the financial detail in the NBR Draft Report (so clearly absent from the Feasibility Study) and identify exactly what fundable business case, if any, lay at the heart of the large body of research data which had been accumulated. Reflecting on this incredible omission in 2011, Perkins' view was simple: "We [Perkins and Symms] were kept at arm's length from the associates." Even with the benefit of nearly 50 years of hindsight, the motivation for maintaining that distance remains a mystery.

It was belatedly agreed at the 18th October meeting – as recommended by the 'associates' – that the directors would commission an independent and searching financial appraisal to substantiate, or otherwise, the original Feasibility Study commissioned by Symes-Schutzmann. It had quickly been concluded by this gathering of expert business and financial advisers – doubtless informed by the Noble Grossart letter of rejection of 15th October – that such an appraisal, taking six months, was an essential pre-requisite to the raising of the necessary financial backing for the project. The 5th February letter notes that, "it was, in the opinion of the associates, absolutely vital to have in hand a report prepared by independent consultants of the highest repute."

Intriguingly, the letter continues that, "At this time [18th October] the associates of B.U.R.C. had no reason to believe that there was an immediate time limit involved in further negotiations with British Railways Board." It would seem that Symes-Schutzmann did not disseminate the content of the pivotal telephone message of 6th October to the associates – and BURCo director Roy Perkins confirms that he knew nothing of the BR ultimatum until receipt of the letter of 4th November. Symes-Schutzmann's motivation is unclear, but with hindsight this looks at the very least like a tactical error, at a time when even a few weeks delay could be critical. Other protagonists vouch that Symes-Schutzmann liked to have matters resolved on his own terms – another example arguably being his complete rejection of BR's proposal for the Border Union trains to terminate at Carlisle Canal station, thereby avoiding the cost of reinstating and maintaining Carlisle No.3 signal box which controlled the access from the West Coast Main Line north of Citadel station to the Waverley Route.

If Perkins was being kept in blissful ignorance of core developments, the Waverley Association support group seems by this stage to have been completely 'out of the loop'. Its Management Committee's 20th October letter to BURCo complained that, "the supposed new edition [of the Feasibility Study] has yet to go to the printers", and stated baldly that they, "feel that we have been deliberately mislead [sic] by the B.U.R. over this fact and we are not prepared to further this deception". The other main bone of contention was that while, "it was agreed at Kensington on May 13th last, that the W.A. would release any news or official views to either the Railway World or the Railway Magazine", Symes-Schutzmann had given his interview to RA Barnes (a personal friend) for the article to be published soon in *Railway World* (having been turned down by the *Railway Magazine*). The signatories concluded that:

> We are now faced with the fact that In December, W.A. members will be able to gain considerably more information about the project from the *Railway World* than we can give them through the Waverley Association newsletter. Members will be asking 'why pay a £1 a year to an association when you can get more information out of a x/- glossy magazine?'

Elevation to the corridors of power

At the sharp end of developments, following formal receipt of the 4th November letter of ultimatum, a BRB / BURCo associates meeting was convened in London on 17th November. This was attended by Willie Thorpe (BRB Deputy Chairman, who had extolled the benefits of closing the Waverley Route when he was General Manager of Scottish Region in 1966), and by Lord Melgund, Michael Lycett and Noel Penny on behalf of the BURCo associates. None of the BURCo directors was in attendance, and it is evident from archive correspondence that by this stage Perkins and Symes-Schutzmann had been effectively side-lined (Symms having withdrawn during the summer). A BR memo records that, "Mr. Thorpe was informed quite categorically that there were no cash resources available at all to meet any of British Rail's claims outlined in [the BR] letter of 4th November".

The detailed BR track diagram which the author has seen indicates that various discrete sections of track totalling $12\frac{1}{2}$ track miles were allocated for sale to BURCo, half from the Down line north of Galashiels, and the other half from the Up line south of Hawick. The age of the rails varied from 1934 to 1966, but fully two thirds of this material was of the modern 'flat bottomed' type, a higher proportion than for the complete track inventory of the Waverley Route within Scottish Region. The appendix to a 5th November 1969 letter from the BRB

The rise and fall of BURCo

Deputy Secretary to BURCo includes quotations for sale of all of the Up line north of Hawick and all of the Down line south thereof, so the 12$\frac{1}{2}$ miles were presumably only spare material to replace life-expired sections on the single line which BURCo had been offered by BR.

Three days before the 17th November London meeting, BURCo associate Hugh McMichael had circulated an agenda for a meeting of the BURCo directors and associates to be held in York on 22nd November. Amongst the 10 Agenda items were:

- The Minutes of the Meeting of Directors-Designate of the North British Railway Company held on 18th October to be approved.

- Lord Melgund to report on the meeting with the Chairman of British Railways Board that week.

- Those present to report on enquiries made to ascertain possible financial support from interested parties after the completion of the [new] feasibility study.

- Consider the letter from British Railways Board to the Chairman dated 4th November 1969, together with the draft contract attached thereto.

However, the York meeting was cancelled, McMichael advising in his letter of 18th November that at the previous day's meeting BRB could not give an immediate decision on whether it could grant the associates "sufficient time to enable a professional feasibility study to be carried out before entering into firm negotiations regarding the acquisition of the Railway".

In a letter to Symes-Schutzmann (copied to Perkins) on 19th November, Lycett admitted that, "I am experiencing a sort of misgiving as though I had pushed the demonstrator of a beautiful new motor car out of the driving seat and taken over myself." He was at pains to emphasise that Melgund and he "both have uppermost in our minds how much the Railway means to you and Roy." Lycett described the meeting with BRB as, "pleasant, and we thought, constructive", but doubted that BRB would give a breathing space for the survey without imposing "crippling interest charges", in which case the associates "must face up squarely to that new problem."

The reaction of Roy Hammond at BR to the situation outlined at the meeting was to describe it as "a very unsatisfactory state of affairs", noting that the suspension of removal of track and equipment was costing BR loss of interest at the rate of about £8,000 per month. He was, however, prepared to recommend to the BR Board that they accept a postponement, provided that by the end of March 1970 BURCo's consultants completed the report needed for final decisions to be made about the future of the project – but interest would accrue from 1st December "on the whole value of the permanent way materials [£885,000]". Lord Melgund's letter of 5th February 1970 to the press records that:

> We asked for a minimum six months grace in which to obtain confirmation of the viability of the Edinburgh – Carlisle line. In the event, we received in a letter following this meeting the offer of four months grace at a cost to us of £8,000 interest charge per month payable to British Railways.

An internal BRB memo of 2nd December from HM Herbert comments that the subsequent reply (from Hugh McMichael on 1st December) to the BRB letter, "holds out no hope whatsoever of the Company being able to meet our interest payments nor does it contain any information about the prospects of the Company raising the necessary funds should the survey be favourable." The memo concludes that, "it seems to me that we must apply the 'coup de grace'".

In the meantime, the *Scotsman* had reported on 26th November 1969 that "British Rail are to begin lifting 34 miles of single-line track on the Edinburgh-Carlisle line later this week", and quoted a BR spokesman as commenting that "I must point out that these tracks are surplus to the requirement of both the British Railways Board and the Border Union Railway Company, who are planning to reopen the line." That same week the *Hawick News*, under a front page headline "Further progress with Waverley line plans", reported the same story and added that "During negotiations for the sale of the line both parties have agreed that the figure be kept confidential but the prospective buyers are said to be 'well pleased' with the asking price." This painted a rosy picture, in stark contrast to what was happening behind the scenes. Just days after the press reports on resumed track-lifting, the 'Up' page of the Hawick Train Register showed one final pencil written note marking the resumption of track-lifting activity (and the last ever train recorded in the book):

> "30-11-69
> Men arrived 7-50am Ballast away for Shankend 8-42am
> Ballast from Millerhill with empty wagons arrived 10-15 am
> away to Newcastleton"

Back at the BRB, a strongly worded and uncompromising draft response to McMichael's 1st December letter was toned down in the final version sent by the Chief Secretary on 5th December, which noted that BRB had been holding material valued at around £¾ million since May and now had to insist on charging interest. Nevertheless Hammond did make a further gesture of co-operation, which had been absent from Herbert's memo and the early draft:

> I am prepared, however, to offer one final solution: it is our view that qualified consultants should be able, within a short period, to undertake a quick appraisal and establish whether or not the venture is worthwhile and that you can comply with our requirements. If that can be done, I would be prepared to recommend to my Board that the interest should not be chargeable until 1st January 1970 instead of 1st December 1969.

BURCo and the Waverley Association – the final rift

Demonstrating the gulf in communication between BURCo and the Waverley Association (WA), a *pro forma* letter from the WA to enquirers – evidently produced in late 1969 – optimistically advised that, 'A draft contract for the purchase of the line was received from the British Railways Board on the 7th. November and negotiations are proceeding satisfactorily'. The WA's November newsletter went further, reporting that, "the Directors of the BURC and the directors designate of the North British Railway Company are well pleased at the price quoted by British Rail." This seems like a deception of the highest magnitude, and one wonders who within BURCo gave the WA such an utterly misleading impression.

In practice, relations between the BURCo directors and the WA had almost completely collapsed. The latter's Management Committee's letter of 13th December – clearly written without any knowledge that the BURCo associates had side-lined the directors some two months earlier – complained that, "we are still awaiting a written reply to the points raised [in our 20th October] letter". Into the bargain, the offending *Railway World* article had been published in the November issue, not December as expected, so the WA Committee had not been able to get the information to members before it appeared in the public domain, and consequently "caused acute embarrassment through the thoughtless action of the very people it was endeavouring to help."

But there was worse to come, concerning, "the number of what have proved to be pieces of false information that have been given to the WA Committee by the Border Union", the first of which (symptomatic of the situation, rather than being important in its own right) concerned the incorrect claim by Symes-Schutzmann that the preserved steam locomotive *Blue Peter* was to be stationed on the railway. The letter continued that, "another piece of misinformation" given to the WA, this time in August, "was that the granting of a Light Railway order was imminent…It now appears that the granting of this order is certainly a considerable way even from now." The Committee Members then raised the key issue not just for the WA / BURCo relationship but more importantly for the project itself:

> A third and very serious misrepresentation has been over finance. From the very outset of the scheme until about six weeks ago the WA has been continually told that finance was not a serious problem and that no difficulty would be experienced in finding a 10% deposit for the line. From facts now in our possession it would appear that the financial problem is one of great magnitude and, from these details, one must draw the rider that the future of the line is by no means assured.

The latter inference was something of an understatement, but the WA was not in a position to be any the wiser. The letter then turned to "the debacle of the [reprinting of the] Feasibility Report in which the WA Committee has been fobbed off with lies and excuses", bemoaning the fact that the corrected edition was "still in the process of being typed on the 8th December!" The Committee had "decided to have nothing further to do with this report", although they were not in a position to know that pulping rather than retyping was the most likely next step by that time anyway. The letter concluded with references to "the apparent breakdown in the flow of information coming from the BUR", and being "perturbed to find that another meeting was held in Edinburgh on the 28th November, apparently in secret." The Committee signed off with the advice that unless it received a full reply to all the points raised in its letters, then it would "deem it necessary to inform the whole of the WA membership as to the facts of the situation, so that they may decide for themselves whether or not the scheme warrants their continued support."

During this period of high drama, the Perkins' archive oscillates between the prosaic and the profound. On 16th December, the solicitor Mark Bonham-Carter wrote to Perkins asking how many copies of the "Memorandum and Articles" should be produced by the printers, and on the same day Major Howard of the Headquarters Scotland (Army) was seeking confirmation that Army Railway Warrants (ie free rail travel on the Border Union Railway) would be acceptable!

BR pulls out of negotiations

Back at the sharp end, on 18th December Hugh McMichael replied on behalf of the BURCo associates to the BRB's 5th December gesture of co-operation, advising, not unreasonably, that in the short period available before imposition of interest charges (just over three weeks) BURCo and associates could not produce the evidence needed to assure their financial advisers. While this letter has not been found in the archives, Melgund's letter of 5th February states that, "We asked for an extension of 14 days until 14 January 1970 during which it was intended to hold a further meeting of B.U.R.C and associates to investigate a further course open to us." Hammond's 23rd December reply on behalf of the BRB was short and to the point:

> It appears to us that no real progress has been made since the meeting with Lord Melgund on 17th November towards obtaining the independent and searching appraisal which was then discussed. In these circumstances the Board must now withdraw the offer to negotiate contained in the letter of 4th November addressed to Mr. Mr. Symes-Schutzmann and will regard themselves as free to dispose of the materials and equipment of the Edinburgh–Carlisle line.

The end of the dream had now been clearly signalled, but the BURCo associates were not ready to call a halt. In his 5th February letter to the press, Melgund stated that he had written privately to the Deputy Chairman of the BRB on 18th December, also asking for an extension until 14th January. He had received a reply "to the effect that although formal negotiations with B.U.R.C. had to be terminated I could rest assured that the door was still open to me to approach British Railways Board within the framework of previous negotiations until 14 January 1970."

One of the last items in Roy Perkins' archive is a 30th December letter from Hugh McMichael to the BURCo directors and associates, advising the recent sequence of events and calling for attendance at critical meetings in London on 8th January 1970. BRB had given way on only one month's interest charge "but suggested that we might ask consultants to make a quick appraisal of our venture to ascertain if it was financially viable." Noel Penny had accordingly arranged for an independent consultant, Mr John Hughes, to discuss the venture with BURCo associates in Edinburgh and with BR in Glasgow:

> Mr. Hughes has now submitted his report to Noel Penny and a copy is being sent to Roy Perkins in order to obtain his comments. I understand that Mr. Hughes is of the opinion that it may be necessary to scale down our venture from what was originally proposed in order to make it financially viable but it would appear that it would be worth spending money on the employment of consultants – provided we can raise the money to pay the consultants fees and the interest charges to British Railways Board from 1st January 1970.

Penny had held a preliminary meeting (about the idea of building a multi-fuel pipeline along the route of the single lifted track) with Burmah Oil "who have expressed considerable interest". It was hoped that at a further meeting (on 8th January) Burmah would agree to pay for a further feasibility study and possibly also the BRB interest charges. McMichael noted that BURCo (strictly speaking BURCo's associates, as the latter were clearly in the initiative) had written to BRB on 18th December asking for a 14-day extension beyond 1st January "to enable us to meet Burmah Oil and ascertain from them if they are prepared to support us financially or not." A reply was still awaited from BRB (although an unofficial agreement to this extension was given later by BRB), but in the meantime the Burmah Oil meeting had been arranged, to be preceded by a meeting of BURCo directors and associates to consider Hughes' report and decide on the line of approach to be adopted with Burmah – this to be followed by a meeting of all directors and associates "in order to take a firm decision on whether to go ahead with this venture or not in order that British Railways Board may be advised without any further delay."

The last throw of the dice

BR was now preparing to make a public announcement that it had broken off negotiations with BURCo. Papers in the personal archive of ex-BR manager Rae Montgomery (now held as part of the North British Railway Study Group archive at the National Records of Scotland in Edinburgh) include a 30th December 1969 BRB Press Office Brief to Alan Clarke, Public Relations & Publicity Officer at Scottish Region, which noted that:

> This is not to be used in its entirety or offered as written. The talking points it makes can be used in discussion, as informally as possible. The important fact to get over is that BRB have been patient and tolerant and that the breakdown has come because there is no proof BURC can meet its obligations.

The Brief continued that, "Because the BURC have been unable, despite long negotiations, to provide any evidence of financial backing, British Rail have withdrawn their offer to negotiate the sale". The formal announcement was made to the press – ironically, exactly a year after the railway had closed – on 6th January 1970. Six days later Hugh McMichael wrote a letter to the associates, marked 'private and confidential', summarising discussions at the two crucial meetings in London on 8th January and subsequent developments. At the second of the two meetings (involving the BURCo associates only) the protagonists had finally accepted the fate of the core project:

> It was agreed by all those present at our meeting that the only course presently open to us was to ascertain from British Rail if we could purchase the land and buildings in order to preserve the 78 miles of route [from Newtongrange to Longtown] for the eventual re-opening of a transport system for the Borders.

BURCo had "no cash to enable us to pay – say £75,000", but at the meeting earlier that day at Castrol House, "had not asked Burmah Oil to finance the purchase of the land and buildings as it was felt preferable that Border Union Railway Co. Ltd. should be the landlords." Instead, "Burmah Oil were asked to put up the necessary finance – say £20,000, to enable a professional feasibility study to be carried out". This was really nine months too late, but the Burmah representatives asked for the consultant John Hughes to comment briefly on three issues, following which they would submit the BURCo proposal to their Board:

(a) The practicability of single line operation [presumably to facilitate the construction and maintenance of the planned fuel pipeline].

(b) Alternative traction methods i.e. Hovertrain, Monorail etc.

(c) A précis of his original report, bearing in mind that we will be starting with nothing except the route and that we will be unable to have a bridge over the A.74 [the MoT having advised that without a £50,000 deposit and bank guarantee for the whole cost by 16th January they could no longer provide a bridge]."

McMichael's letter concluded by impressing on everybody the necessity of keeping all the plans "sub judice": "it would be disastrous if any of the above were leaked to the press at this time. The simple answer to any questions must still be 'No comment'." The archives contain no further references to Burmah Oil and the associated BURCo proposal, but correspondence shows that Lord Melgund did approach the BRB In January and February of 1970 about sale of the land and buildings (excluding track) for £75,000.

However, the revised proposition created some alarm amongst senior officers at BRB, concerned that without adequate financial safeguards, then in the event of BURCo liquidation, the Board would find itself once again liable for maintaining fences, ditches, drains, etc. A memo from PR Dashwood on 14th January noted however that the Deputy Chairman "was evidently showing some reluctance in rejecting the [BURCo associates] proposition." The BRB archives show that at least four draft responses to Melgund were put on paper before the 27th January letter was signed off by Roy Hammond, Chief Secretary of the Board stating that, "this now becomes an ordinary property sale which will be dealt with by the British Rail Property Board".

The letter also made it clear that that the Board was not immediately free to dispose of the land without ministerial consent, and that any offer would have to be considered alongside other interested parties such as local authorities, the National Farmers Union and adjoining property owners. The previous valuation of the land as part of the earlier offer to BURCo would now be "governed by the market" and the Property Board would require "evidence of financial ability to complete the deal [and relieve the Board permanently of its obligations] before commencing negotiations."

Melgund and Hammond then spoke on the phone on 29th January, and the same day the former sent a letter confirming a request for "an inventory of all items for sale as well as ground acreages, etc." Interestingly the letter also noted that:

> The reason for specifically stating that this proposition came from my associates and I, as against the Directors of B.U.R.C. was because we felt that we had done a good deal to get this matter onto a proper business footing and that for that reason and for others you might prefer to deal with us and keep matters on a professional basis.

The implication was clear – Melgund was seeking, albeit very much at the 11th hour, to distance the BURCo associates from the propositions and business plans of the BURCo directors which had failed to convince the BRB and potential investors over the previous 11 months. His subsequent letter to the press on 5th February seemed to protest too much on this point, commenting that:

> …it is to be hoped that no one either now or in the future will have any doubt about the magnificent work which Mr. Symes-Schutzmann and Mr. Perkins, Directors of B.U.R.C., have put into their investigations. Without their initiative and their selfless disregard for the loneliness of giving birth to a brain child there would be no chance whatsoever of an alternative transport system in the Borders in the near future. Win or lose these two men are deserving of our thanks and respect.

Both of the latter directors (and Symms until his withdrawal) had funded their own expenses on behalf of BURCo, but that eulogy for "selfless disregard" was clearly most deserved in the case of Roy Perkins, who gave up his career with Michelin to pursue the railway dream, while Symes-Schutzmann retained his position with the BBC.

The Managing Director of the BR Property Board, CL Smith, advised Hammond in a memo of 30th January that, "it seems to me to be a waste of time to pursue matters with them", and Hammond's reply letter of 4th February to Melgund advised firmly that, "The preparation of the inventory you ask for would be a formidable task which we would not wish to undertake", noting that

The rise and fall of BURCo

BURCo had previously been given plans and had undertaken their own inspections. The letter concluded that:

> I fully appreciate why you, as distinct from the Directors of the Border Union Railway Company, wish to deal with the subject, and that matters should be kept on a professional basis, and it is with this latter thought in mind that I suggested you carry it forward with Mr. C.L. Smith, who is fully informed about this correspondence."

The last letter in the National Archives at Kew from Melgund to BRB was hand written on 5th February, and advised that, "We shall be in touch with your Mr Smith. I am very grateful to you for opening this door to us." It also enclosed a copy of his three-page typed letter of the same date to the press (the final item in the Perkins' archive), which as we have seen incorporated Melgund's detailed clarification and interpretation of the events of the previous few months – designed in part to counter an allegedly confusing statement by a BR spokesman quoted in the *Scotsman* of the previous day.

The letter to the press justified BURCo's associates' change of policy on the grounds that an in-depth independent survey was essential to assess the viability "of any project", and that if the route were to be "owned by B.U.R.C., its associates and supporters, then such a survey can take place in full without impossible deadlines to meet." This was in some ways a reasonable position, but the proposed survey had come far too late in the 13-month period that had elapsed since BURCo had begun hatching its plans. Melgund's letter even made an attempted virtue of the track being lifted as part of any deal, suggesting that the best transport system might turn out to be "a hover train or a mono rail or a gas turbine system."

Sadly, this last desperate throw of the dice had entered the realms of fantasy. The final BR letter in the Kew archive is from Roy Hammond on 6th February, repudiating the allegation of confusing BR statements, and pointing out that, "The time required to evaluate [transport system] alternatives of this nature will be formidable and far more involved than a detailed survey of the property itself." The letter concludes with a warning:

> It is not my intention to release this letter to the press, but should queries arise as a result of your press letter of 5 February I may have to use the contents of this letter and other correspondence.

The penultimate item in the Perkins archive is a letter sent out just four days earlier to all Waverley Association members by the Secretary, Ian Holoran, enclosing a questionnaire in connection with the Committee's decision, "to hold a ballot amongst all its members to ascertain whether the Association should continue or be wound up." The letter noted that following the BRB announcement of 6th January about the end of negotiations, "immediately afterwards the publicity director of the BURC, Mr. David Block, informed the press that a joint BUR/BRB statement would be issued on the 9th January", but that, "*As far as the W.A. Management Committee can ascertain*, the statement for the 9th January has still to be issued" (author's italics).

The letter then set out the project's financial situation, so far as it was known, and advised that BURCo "was having to undertake a complete reappraisal of the scheme...but that it would now probably be at least eighteen months before anything tangible could be seen." Two hundred and seven members were asked to complete and return the questionnaire – and a 9th April 1970 letter in the Ian Holoran archive indicated that, "we had an 84% return on the vote with 74% voting to carry on." The same letter added that, "BURC are just as determined as ever to reopen the line, despite the setbacks", but it was hard to reconcile this view with the evident lack of meaningful progress on the ground.

A long drawn-out demise

The delayed track-lifting task was now free to be completed following BR's withdrawal from negotiations on 23rd December. In his *Scottish Region: A History 1948-73*, AJ Mullay records that:

> In 1970 the January meeting of the Scottish Board considered the disposal of the line's 'assets', following a BRB decision to withdraw from negotiations with an un-named consortium interested in re-opening the Waverley Route. The minutes record that 'Arrangements have now been made to dispose of all assets, other than land and buildings with effect from February 1st'

No archive material has been identified which would clarify whether the BURCo associates (as opposed to directors) seriously pursued the purchase of the line solum beyond February 1970, but there is some circumstantial evidence that a vestigial initiative survived until later that year. The WA's fourth newsletter, dated 18th April 1970 (the day when the author, a WA member, was celebrating his 18th birthday in Inverness) featured – despite the grim reality – a characteristically up-beat message from Bob Symes-Schutzmann, advising "what is happening now":

> To put it quite simply, we are trying to purchase the right of way between Lady Victoria Pit and Longtown so that it may be preserved as a through route. Once

this land is in our possession we are going to commission the independent study which has been required by our financial advisors. This study will show what transport system and what administration is best suited for the area and would prove the most remunerative for its operators and cheapest for its users. With this study completed we shall then approach our backers. It is only if this study proves the line to be a financial viability [sic] that we shall raise the money needed.

One can only wonder if his reference to "a financial viability" was a Freudian slip for "a financial liability". And the reference to "we" – when Symes-Schutzmann had long been side-lined by the associates –provides further confirmation that the realms of fantasy had now been fully entered. The belatedly-encompassed "independent study" should have been undertaken in early 1969 in order to convince BR and potential investors of the viability of a project to purchase and operate *part of the Waverley Route* before the whole project lost all credibility.

The WA newsletter reported the formation of a Scottish Management Committee – to replace the original London-based committee – at a meeting held in Edinburgh on 28th March, at which it was agreed that 13 individuals would contribute to the work of the committee – these including Ian Holoran (liaison with BURCo, "whilst the latters [sic] headquarters remain in London") and Bruce McCartney as Secretary / Treasurer. The newsletter also announced that the WA's *first* AGM would be held on 20th June in Edinburgh at the North Merchiston Boys Club (where the author's father had volunteered in the 1930s).

The Waverley Association – despite the unpropitious circumstances – produced two further newsletters. A single sheet in early June presented accounts showing income of £220 8s 0d and expenditure of £80 0s 4d as at 1st June. The WA's "profit" was a stark contrast to BURCo's complete lack of a business case for a viable railway through the Borders.

When the June 1970 election brought in a Conservative Government, BURCo supporters might reasonably have expected a more favourable ideological audience for the concept of a privately-owned and fully commercial trunk railway. In an adjournment debate in the Commons on 20th July, David Steel referred to the BURCo revised proposal to acquire the railway land with a view to retaining the railway formation for re-opening at some future date:

I hope the Government will again indicate that they will directly, or through British Rail, give every encouragement to this proposal. If the land were sold off piecemeal, there would never again be any possible future use for this through route in the Border region. It is important to keep it intact. The Government claim to be the Government of free enterprise. Here is a free enterprise company. I hope that the Government will give every encouragement in its efforts to retain the railway formation.

The reply from George Younger, the new Under Secretary of State for Scotland (who had publicly argued against closure while in opposition) may have raised false hopes that a Conservative Government would take a fresh and constructive look at BURCo's private enterprise initiative: "I can say that we have so far received no proposals from the Border Union Railway Company. We are only too ready to receive and consider any proposal which it may have in mind." Evidently alarmed by Younger's positive noises, the civil service at the Scottish Office then moved into over-drive. In a 24th July internal memo to his superior JH McGuinness, a JM Howieson was scathing about BURCo – rightly so, by this stage:

> Mr Peeler MOT, Assistant Secretary in Railways Division cannot agree to advising his Parliamentary Secretary to meet the BURC directors with Mr. Younger. His reason is that an offer to meet them will raise false hopes in the public mind of Government assistance which will not, in fact, be available. During their negotiations with BR they were unable to put up a contribution of about £10,000 to cover the legal etc. fees of the transaction or to produce a £$^{1}/_{4}$ m deposit on the sale price of the route. They have obviously no prospect of raising the purchase price; and in the light of that it is difficult to accept that they could purchase rolling stock and operate a viable service. They are, in fact, raising a good deal of false hopes in the Borders which have no chance of materialising and the sooner they can be stopped the better.

The BURCo story then faltered towards what had by then become an inevitable conclusion. The sixth and final Waverley Association newsletter (in late October 1970) reported that in response to Symes-Schutzmann's address to its AGM in Edinburgh on 20th June, the Scottish Management Committee had enrolled no fewer than 150 new members. He had also requested that the WA arrange meetings in the Borders which, according to the newsletter, "would enable the directors to explain their plans to the people intimately involved." Meetings in Gala, Hawick and Newcastleton were duly organised for the 20th and 21st August, only for Symes-Schutzmann to cancel all three in his letter of 11th August, which somewhat mysteriously attributed the cancellation to unspecified "recent developments":

> My counsellors and associates to the Board of Directors to the Border Union Railway Company advise me to ask you, for the time being, to keep very quiet while other approaches are being made…Please believe me, matters are in hand

and are being dealt with very energetically but from a political point of view, we must keep quiet and so must you until a later date.

What did these comments refer to? The archive is virtually silent on this very late period, yet it seems puzzling that Symes-Schutzmann – who had been sidelined by the BURCo associates in October 1969 – now implied that he was back at the heart of the project. Around this time, however, Transport Minister John Peyton decided that BURCo could purchase the line, but only with a five-mile separation from BR metals at each end – a completely unrealistic proposition.

The end of the BURCo dream came not long after the Borders meetings had to be cancelled by Bruce McCartney, the final WA newsletter in October 1970 advising members that:

> The Committee regret to have to inform you that after a meeting of the Scottish Management Committee, on Wednesday, 21st. October, after consultation with the London based Liaison Committee, it has been decided that the Waverley Association should be dissolved.
>
> The total lack of information from the Border Union Railway Company for release to Waverley Association members during the last few months has made it increasingly apparent that the directors of B.U.R.C. have no longer any standing with British Rail over the proposed sale of the Waverley Route between Edinburgh and Carlisle via the Borders. Consequently, the role of the Waverley Association as defined in the Constitution is no longer tenable.

The newsletter also included the WA's final set of accounts, indicating 372 postal orders and international money orders to be refunded to members and supporters, the largest of which, at £24, was the equivalent of £259 today. BURCo's "amateur" support group had had more obvious success in raising funds than its "professional" partner.

Why did BURCo (and its associates) fail?

There are far fewer informed witnesses to the BURCo saga of 1969-70 than to the story of the Waverley Route closure itself. The conventional wisdom amongst railway supporters, enthusiasts and industry people has tended to be that BURCo's failure was due to a combination of unrealistic ambition and a vindictive BR attitude north of the Border – the 1990 *Railway World* article says that, "the eventual failure of the project probably owes more to the Scottish Region of the day than any other factor." But, based on the new evidence unearthed in the research for this book, is that a fair judgement?

There can be no dispute that **the scale of BURCo's ambition** was breathtaking. There was no precedent for the take-over of more than 90 miles of double-track railway as a commercial concern – as opposed to the revival of short branch lines as volunteer-led 'preserved' railways. A measure of their ambition is that it took until the Weardale Railway re-opening in 2010 for a British standard-gauge heritage railway to introduce an all-day year-round public-transport train service – and this 16-mile operation lasted only 18 months before withdrawal through lack of patronage. Even the longest preserved line in current existence (the West Somerset Railway) is less than a quarter of the length that BURCo sought to operate – although to be fair, BURCo was aiming to be an all-year commercial railway rather than a seasonal volunteer-dominated operation. But there is no question that the scale of the project was monumental in relation to the immediate resources available; and the recurring letters in 1969 (from BR and others) expressing concern about delays in replying, do underline at a prosaic level the size of the task taken on by just three directors, two of whom were only working part-time on behalf of BURCo – and one of these two had effectively dropped out of the initiative by the summer of 1969.

Reflecting on events in 2011, Roy Perkins wondered whether his sentimental attachment (through family connections) to the Hawick-Carlisle section prevented him from adopting a more hard-nosed preference for a project based on Hawick-Edinburgh, which might have stood more chance of success. This is hard to judge, even in hindsight, since, while the northern section undoubtedly offered vastly more all-year passenger potential, it would still have required a monumental transformation in circumstances for this to become a commercially viable operation no longer dependent on Government subsidy – but perhaps with the tourism and steam add-ons, and the greater flexibility which private sector operation brought, it might conceivably have been realisable. An alternative view is that a largely volunteer-run steam operation, initially from Hawick to Newcastleton (with Newcastleton to Longtown 'mothballed'), could have created a breathing space for the major timber prospects to be developed. But this is no more than conjecture.

BURCo's business planning strategy was clearly inadequate for the task of demonstrating a convincing **business case** for the financial viability (without grant subsidy) of a Borders rail re-opening scheme. The Feasibility Study delivered in August 1969 was far from being a sufficiently robust document to convince BR or potential investors, and by the time the BURCo directors and associates had acknowledged this – in October – BR had run out of patience over the time and money spent on dealing with the company. Had a more robust and quantitative study been commissioned in the spring of 1969, then a core commercial basis (supported by volunteer labour) for re-opening at least part of the Waverley Route might have been identified in sufficient time to keep BR on board while investors were still being courted.

However, the sheer scale of the transformation of costs and revenues required to make the railway viable without Government grant aid does suggest that for the complete BURCo plan to have succeeded would have required an optimum outcome in every contributory strand of the project – external funding, purchase price from BR, running powers over BR metals, ongoing cost-effectiveness and reliability of rolling stock, exceptional passenger traffic growth, etc. With hindsight it does not seem credible that all these pieces of the jigsaw could have fallen neatly into place. The full BURCo proposal now looks like a classic case of 'here's something we'd love to do – now how can we justify it?', rather than, 'here is a set of problems – so what are the potential solutions?'

Interviews with protagonists point to **the internal dynamic of BURCo and BURCo's external presentation** being factors in alienating some potential support, but it can be hard to disentangle this from the inevitable bitterness felt afterwards by a variety of individuals who had invested much faith and hope (and in the case of the South of Scotland Chamber of Commerce, more than £1,000) in the project.

Nevertheless, references to BURCo quickly becoming the "Bob Symes-Schutzmann show" pinpoint an added difficulty, in part associated with the fact that the scheme was essentially South of England-based, notwithstanding Roy Perkins' very strong family connections with the Newcastleton area and his domicile there for much of 1969. Perkins and Symms were both in their early twenties (but with business backgrounds), whereas Symes-Schutzmann was in his forties but had no business experience. For all the latter's energy, innovative ideas and consummate skills amongst 'the old boys network', his domination of the Board of Directors and his style of management appear to have been a weakness at the heart of the project. In his undoubted presentational drive, he had evidently neglected – until it was too late – to listen carefully to others, including Perkins, who had more experience and expertise in business and marketing.

In discussion with the author in 2011, Symes-Schutzmann conceded that, "I may have been dictatorial, but I was flying solo" – he was evidently happy to leave the financial analysis to Perkins, so that he could concentrate on the networking to secure finance. However, the failure to fully involve the 'associates' of BURCo – with their wide range of business and financial skills – until it was too late, must rank as one the worst shortcomings of the project, but Symes-Schutzmann has pointed out that this was a difficult period for the British economy, and some of the associates' own businesses were struggling.

The *Railway World* article of December 1990 suggested that **the existence and demeanour of the Waverley Association** (WA) had been a key problem:

> In the event and unintentionally, the WA played a significant part in the scheme failing. Plenty of officials were still having problems coming to terms with the privatisation concept presented by the BUR. With the arrival of the fairly vociferous WA they recognised a familiar animal, the preservationist, and firmly pigeonholed the whole project as preservation, doubtless with a sigh of relief!

In discussion with the author in 2011, Symes-Schutzmann remained adamant that the WA was a problem, muddying the waters around the business proposition, and giving BR and private companies such as Burmah Oil an excuse to caricature the whole exercise as 'playing at trains.' However, Ian Holoran, formerly Secretary of the WA, disputed this version of events:

> So far as Bob Symes-Schutzmann's allegation that his association with the WA torpedoed his ambition, his argument has been sunk by virtue of the fact that he failed while many subsequent 'enthusiast' preservation attempts have been successful. Ironically, his original idea of a professional business run on commercial lines with the help of volunteers has now become common practice among the larger preserved railways.

The overall intelligence gathered for this book suggests that Symes-Schutzmann did indeed attribute too much blame to the support group, part of a wider narrative which blamed others – while not conceding that BURCo had gone about anything in the wrong way. At the end of the day it is hard to avoid the conclusion that it was BURCo's absence of a convincing business plan, far more than any misperceptions created by the WA, which destroyed the project. In fairness to Symes-Schutzmann, in discussion with the author in 2011 he conceded that, "of course, I did make mistakes – with hindsight I should have used better financial contacts."

The *Railway World* article's interpretation and analysis of events – and conclusions on why the project failed – too often read like a whitewash of the BURCo directors (and implicitly Symes-Schutzmann in particular). Rather than the WA being significantly to blame, it would appear from archive evidence and discussion with some of the key protagonists, that it was very poorly treated, being kept so much in the dark as to what was happening at the core of the project that it could not possibly fulfil its potential as an important support body for BURCo. It seems highly unfortunate that the business skills of John Grant were not brought to bear directly on BURCo, rather than being restricted to the enthusiast support activities of the Waverley Association.

Archive research has unearthed a mixed picture on **the BR attitude to the sale**. The British Railways Board in London, and London Midland Region, appear to have been largely co-operative (and the latter even enthusiastic) throughout most of 1969, with the former possibly partly having an eye on the public relations implications and the latter perhaps motivated by the prospects for additional long-haul revenue generated by travellers heading for an interchange with the Border Union at Carlisle. The Scottish Region was much less positive throughout the whole BURCo saga, and may well have been determined to avoid being 'shown up' by a private company.

The BRB archives at Kew suggest that the Board was in fact remarkably patient with BURCo and its associates, given the very long period of time over which the prospective purchasers failed to deliver a convincing business case or evidence of financial backing. Certainly, old attitudes may still have been pervasive, in contrast to the situation just three years later when the Paignton-Kingswear line transferred seamlessly into the hands of its present operator – but in fairness the latter was only six miles long, an enthusiast railway based on tourism, and as such an entirely different proposition from a 98-mile secondary main line.

While the Board's sale offer of 6th October 1969 to BURCo can be seen as onerous and unreasonably expensive, it may well have been designed to bring matters to a head, as senior BRB officers became increasingly exasperated at BURCo's continuing failure to deliver while the Board's realisable assets remained rusting on the ground. The now unearthed archive evidence – contrary to the received wisdom since 1970 – does not therefore suggest that the finger can be pointed at BR as a key factor in the demise of BURCo.

One of the most intriguing aspects of the BURCo story is **the Government attitude to the sale**. Archive research suggests that neither Labour in its 1969-70 administration nor the 1970-74 Conservative Government were enthusiastic about the project. The Labour attitude might be understandable, given that in those days the party was overtly in favour of public rather than private enterprise, but the lack of Conservative interest is a continuing puzzle.

Even Bob Symes-Schutzmann, when quizzed by the author at the 2009 AGM of the Campaign for Borders Rail, was unable to come up with an explanation as to why a Government so committed to private enterprise lacked much evident enthusiasm for the BURCo project – although the *realpolitik* may simply have been that by the time the Conservative Government was in place, BURCo and its associates had lost all credibility with both the public and private sectors. This was quite a contrast to the later story of the Settle & Carlisle line, where after five years of attempting to close the line the Conservative Government decided in

1988 to try to sell it, principally as a tourist attraction. As Stan Abbott and Alan Whitehouse wrote in *The Line that Refused to Die* (1994 edition):

> Lazard Brothers, the merchant bank appointed by BR to handle the sale, had produced a glossy and expensive looking 45-page brochure, complete with colour photographs, for potential buyers. It was astonishing how attractively the line – said by BR to be run down and obsolete – could be portrayed in what amounted to an overgrown set of estate agent's particulars.

In a wonderful irony, BR then sabotaged efforts to sell the line by blocking the possibility of private trains operating on the key connecting route to Leeds from Hellifield, and eventually issued its own brochure extolling the attractions of "the most scenic main line in England". The Waverley Route might not have been the most scenic line in Scotland – to be fair, the competition was pretty tough – but with the right marketing it could have become a very popular attraction, just as the S&C has done since finally being reprieved from closure.

BURCo's big problem was that the section of the route which would generate all-year revenues (Hawick-Edinburgh) was not the same section which offered the best steam tourism or indigenous freight opportunities (Hawick-Carlisle). Had all these markets coincided on 40 or 50 miles of rail route, the scale of the challenge – while still enormous – would have been more manageable.

Unfortunately BURCo was stuck with the economic geography of the Borders as it found it in 1969, and, ironically, its best chance might have been if the whole of the Waverley Route had *not* been available for potential purchase. Had Richard Marsh reprieved Hawick-Edinburgh, then a single track line from Hawick could have been developed for steam tourist traffic over the 20 wild miles to Newcastleton, with the route from there to Longtown (and onwards on BR metals) used initially for outbound timber traffic and eventually for special trains from the BR network, as Hawick-Newcastleton steam became a growing national attraction. But Marsh did not reprieve Hawick-Edinburgh; BURCo failed; and unfortunately in the process the expectations of too many people in the Borders and beyond (including the author) were raised far too high – only to be bitterly dashed.

Overall, it can simply be concluded that the BURCo dream was, in the end, a fantasy.

Hawick to Carlisle
abandoned to the track-lifters

Track lifting on the Waverley Route (which began south of Hawick on 7th January 1969) was suspended between March and November 1969 while BR awaited the outcome of discussions with BURCo. Lonely Shankend is untouched on 24th May 1969, with double track, crosssover, Up refuge siding and signal box (opened in 1916) still in situ. The box remains to this day (in private ownership), having been restored as a holiday home in the the 1990s. *Ian Holoran*

Shankend Down distant signal and Bridge 197, looking north on 24th May 1969. The man investigating the signalling mechanism is thought to be Chris Golding of the Waverley Association. Accommodation bridges for livestock, such as this one, were a characteristic feature of the Waverley Route south of Hawick. *Ian Holoran*

The Golden Bridge south of Whitrope is a substantial structure, built to last: it still survives, with the B6399 Hawick to Newcastleton road passing under the old railway structure, seen here on 25th May 1969, with the two gents striding along the track thought to be Roy Perkins of BURCo and his father. It was known as the Golden Bridge on account of its large construction cost, allegedly "every brick costing a guinea". *Ian Holoran*

The early phase of lifting the Up line south of Hawick left untouched the more complex task of removing the track from Whitrope Tunnel. The remaining section can just be seen, poking from the northern portal of the tunnel on 24th May 1969. *Ian Holoran*

Another accommodation bridge – Bridge 204, beside Stichel Hill – dominates the scene as the railway drops down at 1 in 75 from Whitrope Summit to Riccarton Junction. Looking south on 25th May 1969.
Ian Holoran

Bridge 205 and Riccarton Up Distant frame the site of Riccarton North box, closed in 1959 but not demolished until the late 1960s.
Ian Holoran

It took a photographer with a head for heights (and surely with no authorisation from BR!) to capture the railway panorama from Riccarton Up Distant signal post on 25th May 1969. The barrow crossing in the foregound linked the Down side cess to Riccarton North box. *Ian Holoran*

A laden trolley stands forlornly on the Down line adjacent to Riccarton box on 25th May 1969. This view taken from a signal post shows that most of the former 33 railway houses at the isolated settlement had already been demolished. Towards the end of rail services, in 1968-69, just two dwellings were occupied by a total of four residents, and after January 1969 all but one person moved out. *Ian Holoran*

Riccarton Down Home signal and another accommodation bridge are seen in this view looking north on 25th May 1969. *Ian Holoran*

Lifting of the Up line at Steele Road had come to a halt several months before this 25th May 1969 shot, looking south. This was the favoured territory for Peter Handford's classic Argo Transacord sound recordings of trains battling up the eight miles of continuous 1 in 75 gradient from north of Newcastleton to north of Riccarton Junction. Handford's ashes were scattered at the site of Steele Road station following his death in 2007. *Ian Holoran*

A timber permanent way hut dominates the otherwise empty landscape scene looking north towards Steele Road station on 25th May 1969. *Ian Holoran*

The Up line had been lifted several months prior to this 25th May 1969 photo, looking north through Bridge 254 towards the Liddel Viaduct and Newcastleton. *Ian Holoran*

The Waverley Route bridge over the Kershope Burn which here forms the Scotland/England boundary, seen from the east on 25th May 1969. *Ian Holoran*

The lofty Bridge 243 carried the B6318 Haltwhistle-Langholm road over the Waverley Route a half-mile south of Penton Station. Although located in England, the railway section from Kershope Foot to Riddings Junction stayed under BR Scottish Region control until closure. The bridge, seen here looking south on 26th May 1969, still stands. *Ian Holoran*

By 26th May 1969, the Up line through Bridge 244 just north of Ridings Junction had gone, lifted before the suspension of track recovery works in March. *Ian Holoran*

Captured from a signal gantry, looking north, a traditional railway goods yard scene survives at Longtown on 25th May 1969. The depot would remain in operation until August 1970, when the former Waverley Route section from Longtown to the RAF Brunthill connection south of Harker was also closed completely. *Ian Holoran*

A close-up of Longtown goods shed, at the north end of the Up platform on 25th May 1969.
Ian Holoran

On 25th May 1969, Longtown goods yard featured a mix of coal and general merchandise traffic. The left-hand siding would be used for a BURCo / BR timber loading trial in November of that year.
Ian Holoran

The Up platform at Longtown was dominated by a substantial water tower, see here on 25th May 1969. *Ian Holoran*

On 25th May 1969, the water column and hose beside the Up line at Longtown station still survived from the steam era. The last-recorded steam-hauled train through Longtown was on 14th November 1967, when Britannia Class No. 70022 Tornado substituted for a failed diesel on the 19.44 Carlisle-Edinburgh passenger service. *Ian Holoran*

The old and the new clash at Longtown on 25th May 1969. *Ian Holoran*

Two distant signals (the left-hand one the Down Distant for Longtown) and Bridge 253 are captured looking north on 25th May 1969. Note the concrete sleepers on the Down track and the combination of wooden sleepers and flat-bottomed rail on the Up. *Ian Holoran*

Lyneside signal box (on the Down side) and former station building, seen on 25th May 1969. The box and the Up line would close in August 1969, and the Down line in August 1970. Lyneside station had closed to passenger traffic as early as 1929, one of the few stations on the Waverley Route not to survive until 6th January 1969
Ian Holoran

No architectural awards for the Up side shelter at Parkhouse Halt, seen on 25th May 1969. The station – opened in 1941 to serve war workers at nearby RAF Kingstown, and never listed in public timetables – had a working life of less than 28 years.
Ian Holoran

CHAPTER 3

The lingering death of the railway

After a hiatus of six months BR track-lifting activity resumed in November 1969 – and, with prospects for the railway's return fast diminishing, it was not long before alternative uses for the rail solum were being mooted. The National Archives of Scotland contain a substantial body of Scottish Office / Ministry of Transport correspondence from 1970 around the politically sensitive issue of disposing of parts of the Hawick-Edinburgh formation, to facilitate new road construction, well before the end of the two-year moratorium (imposed by Richard Marsh when announcing the closure consent in 1968) on 6th January 1971.

By 25th February 1970, reference was being made within the Scottish Office to "5 sections of the above line where considerable savings of Government money [on road building] could be effected if the formation were to be given up by BR". These were in Galashiels, Tweedbank, east of Melrose, north of Newtown St Boswells and in Hawick. During the next month this issue was propelled to almost the highest level possible. On 25th March, Albert Murray, Parliamentary Secretary at the MoT, wrote to Dickson Mabon, the Under Secretary of State for Scotland, to the effect that:

> I think it is now quite clear that there is no question of the restoration of a service on the line in the near future by a private company…In this connection I should mention that the clerk of Roxburgh County Council has written to the Department asking whether it is still necessary to build a bridge to span the railway for the new section of the A6091 at Tweedbank. *Use of the formation would considerably reduce costs in this respect.* (author's italics)

By 8th May, Dickson Mabon – having specifically excised an earlier draft's specific reference to the sensitive moratorium – was strongly emphasising the cost advantages in a letter to Albert Murray which stated that *"quite substantial savings in road expenditure could be achieved by using parts of the formation for road works."* (author's italics) An undated Scottish Office advisory note to Roxburgh County Council referred to the Scottish Economic Planning Board's meeting of 28th May, when they decided to recommend that the restriction on disposal of track formation be lifted, with this recommendation to be considered by the incoming Government after the General Election of 18th June. The confidential debate about the moratorium was now moving towards a conclusion which would effectively set the seal on hopes for reinstatement of rail services in the foreseeable future. In a draft JH McGuinness memo of 8th June it was noted that:

> Use of the rail bed in the work of constructing that part of the new A6091 link road between A7 and A68 along the southern part of the Tweedbank site *would probably result in time saving of only one month and financial saving of some £10,000*…The [Scottish Economic Planning] Board felt, nevertheless, that the psychological advantage to be derived from freeing the formation now for this purpose and so imparting a sense of urgency to the development of the area should be utilised especially in view of the delay which has already occurred. (author's italics)

Only the formalities were left, and a subsequent draft memo from Dickson Mabon to Albert Murray stated "you will no doubt wish to tell the Railways Board that they can proceed with a disposal application." Ironically, the "psychological" dimension – which had been invoked by the Scottish Economic Planning Board in June 1967 to resist closure of the railway – was now, three years later, being used to justify a road breaching the continuity of the rail corridor, for the sake of very modest material advantage. This was to be a precedent which would result in piecemeal destruction of key sections of the solum of the Waverley Route over the next 30 years – adding to the cost and complexity of eventual reinstatement between Edinburgh and Tweedbank, and posing particular problems for any further southwards extension through a high concentration of road breaches between Tweedbank and the south side of St Boswells.

Track-lifting now moved into top gear. On 1st April 1970, BR ran an Inspection Saloon hauled by Birmingham Type 2 (aka Class 26) No. D5307 south of Hawick – according to Robert Robotham in *The Waverley Route – the Postwar Years*, "to allow contractors to bid for demolition work". Bruce McCartney recollects an amusing incident that day:

> Having been tipped off about this special working, I turned up at Stobs to take a photo, and approaching the station from the footbridge I had this exchange with

The lingering death of the railway

a man walking his dog further up the line towards Shankend, on the track itself. I shouted 'There's a train coming!', to which he replied 'Huntie gouk' [English translation: 'April Fool']. Seconds later, there was the sound from both the Type 2 diesel and the rusty track being scrunched. I took my photo facing the Hawick direction, then turned round to look up towards Shankend, and watched the gent scrambling up the track verge. As he later approached me after the train had passed, he mumbled, 'Ye bugger, ye were right!'

The Waverley Association's fourth newsletter (in April 1970) reported that:

> The running of the train after British Rail's refusal to permit the BURC to have an inspection trolley run over the line has brought angry criticism from several sections of the Borders Communities. Mr. David Steel, M.P. for Roxburgh, Selkirk and Peebles, has put down a question in the House of Commons for the Minister of Transport regarding the incident.

BR has (temporary) second thoughts?

There is some dispute over whether around this time BR had second thoughts about closing the line completely. The July 1970 issue of *Modern Railways* carried a short news item which reported that:

> Following approval for the Weaver Junction-Glasgow electrification, there are indications that BR may have reopening of the Waverley route from Carlisle to Edinburgh in mind. The immediate use would be as a diversionary route during electrification, but it is understood that BR representatives have also been actively canvassing the potential for new revenue-earning traffic should the line be restored.

The report also stated that, "it is alleged" that BR were exploiting the ground work and surveys undertaken by BURCo, in particular in relation to some 300,000 tons of timber a year. It is unclear who the source of these reports was, but *Modern Railways* cited as evidence for the "belief that re-opening is now contemplated", track-lifting being confined to singling, and a recent run over the rationalised route by a Hallade Track Recording car. The Waverley Association's fourth newsletter reported that:

> …it has been reliably reported that recently a track recording vehicle has been run over the line on a number of occasions. This news, coupled with the announcement of the Crewe-Glasgow electrification project has added strength

to the rumour that B.R. is considering the line as an alternative route at least during the period of installation of the electrification.

The Waverley Association's sixth (and final) newsletter in October 1970 commented that:

> ...the retention of a single line between Longtown and Hawick, and double track between Hawick and Edinburgh, after completion of lifting redundant material on the southern section gives backing to the much quoted statement, albeit unconfirmed, that B.R. are retaining the Waverley Route as a possible diversionary line when electrifications starts between Glasgow and Carlisle in May 1971.

While ex-BR manager Rae Montgomery in 2011 recollected this as having been a definite (but short-lived) proposal, others were less sure. Ex BR-manager Allan McLean reflected that:

> I joined BR shortly after all this, and the idea of using the Waverley Route for diversions never came up at the meetings I was involved in on the Weaver Junction/Glasgow electrification, but maybe the idea had been put to rest before I joined in the summer of 1970?

David Prescott (who joined BR in 1974 and ultimately became a senior manager in the industry) had his doubts, wondering if this may have been a "fishing trip" by someone with an idea, as opposed to a BR policy. He also pointed out that the West Coast electrification included a massive downgrade of the Carlisle-Dumfries-Kilmarnock-Glasgow line after its use as a diversionary route including closure of one section (Dalry-Kilmarnock) and singling of others – "so I cannot see any official view looking to re-open a parallel route."

Bruce McCartney was surprised that he had never heard reports about the alleged Hallade Track Recording car, as "there was a very active group of Hawick enthusiasts who ought to have 'clocked' this" – and this view was echoed by Hawick resident and rail enthusiast Ian Bell. However, as the Hallade track recorder was in fact a piece of portable equipment, it could have been conveyed on the 1st April Inspection Saloon observed (and photographed) by Bruce McCartney, but research could neither prove nor disprove this theory.

McCartney also noted that 15 months before the *Modern Railways* article, BR had refused to run a rugby special from Hawick to Edinburgh, as the signalling was not up to passenger standards, but that of course pre-dated the go-ahead for electrification, and management attitudes may have shifted over this period.

The lingering death of the railway

The jury is probably still out on this little-known story – on balance, the author's view (possibly influenced by wishful thinking) is that it may well have been a genuine BR proposal, as the diversionary advantages would have been significant, and the timber prospects were strong and had been undergoing serious examination by BR in late 1968. After three to four years of testing the latter market over a single-track railway, with perhaps just one or two intermediate signal boxes between Edinburgh and Carlisle, and restricted to 40 mph – which still would have been fast enough for a time advantage for diverted passenger trains on Saturdays and Sundays – BR could then have reviewed the position after the West Coast Main Line was fully upgraded.

Presumably however, the sheer cost of maintaining, as well as operating, over 90 miles of railway – for perhaps just one or two timber trains over the southern half daily (Monday to Friday) and single numbers of diverted trains daily on Saturdays and Sundays – would have been deemed to be an unviable proposition for a nationalised industry very much strapped for cash. As Bernard Lamb suggested to the author in 2012, the answer may lie in the 220-plus BR files on WCML electrification at the National Archives in Kew…

On the surviving eight-mile section of the Waverley Route south of Longtown, freight services over the short stretch between Stainton Junction (just south of Kingmoor Yard) and Canal Junction in Carlisle (including a major bridge over the River Eden) were withdrawn in August 1969. At the same time, the Up line was closed between Longtown and the connection to the Brunthill RAF 14 Maintenance Unit, one mile north of Stainton Junction, and signal boxes were closed at Lyneside, Brunthill and Canal Junction.

By August 1970 a facing crossover had been installed at Mossband Junction on the West Coast Main Line and the single line thence to the MoD Depots at Longtown and Smalmstown converted from Up-only working to bi-directional. The line from Longtown to Brunthill was closed completely in August (thereby avoiding a bridge requirement for the new M6), together with Longtown ground frame and freight depot, and MoD trains began running direct from Kingmoor over the Mossband crossover which might have carried re-routed Waverley Route passenger trains, had a more enlightened strategy been developed during the early 1960s.

The one mile stub of the Waverley Route from Stainton Junction to the Brunthill RAF 14 MU depot survived as a long freight siding; 14 MU closed in 1997, but a new road-rail distribution depot for Carlisle Warehousing was built on the old Waverley Route solum, and subsequently has received steel, fertiliser and cement by train. This and the short stretch from Millerhill to Portobello Junction are the only sections of the former main line still carrying freight (as the latter is effectively barred from the new Borders Railway).

Last-gasp efforts

On 2nd June 1971, the *Hawick News* reported that proposals by Lord Melgund – who had written thoughtfully about the Beeching Report in the same paper in 1963, and more recently had been an associate of BURCo – to have the route of the railway protected for future service to the Borders had been rejected by the County Council. In a comment which looked visionary (in the absence this time of his previous mention of hover trains), Melgund – who was to become Convener of Borders Regional Council from 1990 until 1996 – had said that, "It appeared that the time would come when some other mode of transport would become necessary which would require a north/south route for which the rail-line was the only possible route."

It was reported that Lord Melgund and his associates had found financiers who would be willing to consider the purchase of the Waverley Route. However, before any authority could be obtained to commence a survey of the route, "those involved would require a firm assurance that the Waverley route would remain intact at least for the period of two years or so which would be required to carry out the survey." Melgund and his associates had been rebuffed by the Scottish Office: "The Under Secretary of State for Development had refused to consider the proposals further or to give a hearing to Lord Melgund and his associates and had stated that the roads in the Borders would be adequate until 1980." Unfortunately, Roxburgh County Council had the same poverty of vision, and "the sub-committee agreed that the County Council should not make any representations to the Scottish Office or to British Rail about the disposal of the Waverley line."

Despite the inexorable retreat northwards and southwards of the remaining track, occasional correspondents to the *Scotsman* still made the case for the revival of the railway. Provost Pate of Galashiels, having long adjusted to an alternative transport future for the Borders, was brusquely dismissive in a letter of 27th July 1971:

> To endeavour to resurrect [Border railways] in the face of the very competition which killed them would be folly of the first degree...The 90-mile strip of railway track from Edinburgh to Carlisle constitutes a barrier to progress, tolerable so long as it served a useful purpose but now a hindrance to development on every hand. The railway is dead and far beyond revival. The sooner this fact is accepted and acted upon by all concerned the sooner will its track be available for the promotion of industry, tourism and agriculture. The sooner, too, will we have a straightening of roads, a realignment of bridges and a freer flow of traffic. To cry over the past is no way in which to face the future.

The lingering death of the railway

Pate was to be proved right about the fate of the railway (at least until the 21st century), and the programme of track removal steadily eliminated the iron road from the Central Borders. BR papers in the personal archive of ex-BR manager Rae Montgomery (now held as part of the North British Railway Study Group archive at the National Records of Scotland in Edinburgh) indicate that on 4th August 1971 the Secretary of State for the Environment advised that he had no objection to disposal of the formation south of Lady Victoria Colliery to the London Midland boundary at Riddings, qualified by one mundane and two tantalisingly mysterious exceptions:

> certain interests of the Burgh of Galashiels (removal of railway bridge over Wheatland Road) Leyland Gas Turbines (part of the formation for experimental test bed purposes) and I.C.I. (utilising Whitrope Tunnel) should be borne in mind.

Meanwhile, moves to make alternative use of the solum gathered pace. On 1st March 1972 the *Scotsman* reported that, "negotiations have started with the estates department of British Rail and local authorities in the Borders for the sale of the former Edinburgh-to-Carlisle railway line." Both Galashiels and Hawick town councils had said they wanted to acquire all railway land in their respective burghs – for factories, roads and, in the case of Hawick, a sports complex – and "expect to be in possession of the land they want within 12 months."

In September of the same year, the Countryside Commission for Scotland published *Disused Railway Lines in Scotland: a Strategic Appraisal*, which noted in the case of the Waverley Route that, "despite great efforts by the Scottish Development Department to find alternative uses for the line, it has aroused only piece-meal interest." It was suggested that, "on the assumption that a decision were ultimately made to extend the Pennine Way northwards towards the Central Belt of Scotland…[the Waverley Route] should be examined for sections which could usefully contribute to a long distance path."

The last tracks are lifted

Back on the retreating railway – according to reports in the *Railway Observer* newsletters of the Railway Correspondence & Travel Society – on 6th November 1970 a number of local papers had carried a notice issued by British Railways warning persons living in the vicinity of the line to beware of trains which would be operating from 16th November for a period of 20 weeks in connection with track-lifting.

A film report on the BBC television news programme *Reporting Scotland* on 19th November showed scenes of track-lifting in progress – a belated reminder of the line's significance well beyond the Borders. An unidentified Class 08 shunter travelled light to Hawick on 16th January 1971, the first movement noted for many months, and Birmingham Type 2 (aka Class 26) No. D5304 – happily now preserved on the Bo'ness & Kinneil Railway – was seen on a track recovery train on the 18th. On 21st March English Electric Type 4 (aka Class 40) No. D286 was observed at Heriot with a load of recovered track heading towards Edinburgh. The train crew evidently had considerable difficulty in opening the level crossing gates as a heavy fall of snow had been cleared by road snow ploughs and piled up against the gates.

While D286 did not escape the breaker's torch, analysis of two sources – 'Diesel locomotives known to have worked into or through Hawick' (KA Gray, unpublished, 2009) and *Preserved locomotives of British Railways* (Pritchard and Hall, Platform 5 Publishing Ltd, 2016) – reveals that all seven preserved Class 40s traversed the Waverley Route during their working lives on BR. Remarkably, some 69 locos – of 12 different classes – which are known to have worked into or through Hawick are now in preservation, including 18 Class 47s, 12 of the 13 preserved Class 26s, 10 of the 12 preserved BR Type 4s (aka Class 45), all three preserved Class 46s and the sole surviving Clayton Type 1.

The author was subsequently astonished to discover – by consulting *British Railways Pocket Book No. 1: Locomotives 2018* (Pritchard and Hall, Platform 5 Publishing Ltd, 2017) – that some 43 former Hawick visitors remain in commercial service on the main-line network: all being Class 47s, 57s or 37s, principally operated by West Coast Railways (headquarters in Carnforth) or Direct Rail Services (headquarters in Carlisle). The Waverley Route certainly witnessed traction built to last.

Back on the shrinking former main line, specific track-lifting dates – when both the Up and Down tracks were lifted – shown on the BR diagram are 3rd December 1970 at Milepost 81 just north of Penton, through to 10th February 1972 at Milepost 18 (Falahill). Much of this work was unseen by the wider public (and certainly unsung), but there was at least one observer of the last train to cross the prominent Teviot Viaduct just south of Hawick station – a northbound track recovery service on 18th April 1971, hauled by Class 08 shunting locomotive No. D3880. It appears that this 14-month phase of lifting ceased at Milepost 15 on Borthwick Bank, and then recommenced there as late as 5th September 1972 but there are no dates written on the track diagram thereafter. A 530-yard section lifted in October 1971 a mile north of Gala station (on the Down line) was, ironically, one of the early sections of continuously-welded rail (CWR) installed in Scotland: in 1962, three years before CWR became standard for all main-line relaying across BR.

The lingering death of the railway

BR papers in the personal archive of ex-BR manager Rae Montgomery (now held as part of the North British Railway Study Group archive at the National Records of Scotland in Edinburgh) include a 6th January 1971 memo from Scottish Region's Assistant General Manager requesting BRB authority to recover the second track between Millerhill Yard and Lady Victoria Pit and convert the signalling for the remaining single track to 'one train working', at an estimated surplus of £283,527, allowing for contractor outlays and valuation of recoverable materials. It was estimated that work would be completed by December 1971, but in practice coal traffic from Lady Victoria only survived until that month, when the remaining branch was cut back to the Newbattle Coal Preparation Plant at Butterfield a short distance to the north – and this in turn succumbed to complete closure in June 1972.

In *Scottish Region: A History 1948-1973*, AJ Mullay commented that a more enlightened BR attitude to rural public transport would have "eliminated the exaggerated and sometimes downright misleading estimates of the value of recoverable material from closed lines". An appendix to his book indicates that the BR Scottish Board Meeting Minutes for January 1971 recorded a figure of £283,527 (£3,831 per route mile) for what "appears to give a net figure for recovery" of track between Riddings and Lady Victoria Colliery, although the author has warned that these BR records must be treated with caution. Certainly, as the last stretch of track was not lifted until the following year, BR must have had an extremely good deal with the track-lifting contractors, or a crystal ball.

Of the total track mileage of 148½ miles recovered by Scottish Region (ie from the very south end of Millerhill Yard to the LMR boundary at Riddings), 54% was re-used elsewhere on the BR network, the rest presumably going for scrap. One prosaic aspect of the redeployment of track is that sections of modern flat-bottomed rail were re-used for sidings at Kincardine power station – but when the power station closed in 1997, the SRPS acquired the rails for the Bo'ness & Kinneil Railway. Some of the old Waverley Route lives on by the shores of the Forth.

But back in late 1972, after 110 years of passenger and freight operation, four months of vestigial freight, and nearly four years of start-and-stop track-lifting, the last remnants of railway had vanished from the abandoned Waverley Route. As civil servant Frank Spaven (the author's father) had warned at the Scottish Office in 1965, closure had rendered the Borders region:

> by far the largest population grouping in Britain with no accessible railway services…the population in this area who will be more than 25 miles by road from the nearest railway station will amount to 70,000 persons.

BURCo: its Directors, brand, and sole railway operation

At Saturday's Border Rail Press conference are, (left to right): Mr Roy Perkins, Mr Martin Symms, and Mr Bob Symes-Schutzmann.

Rail plan impresses Borderers

Local authorities in the Borders were asked yesterday to support plans for reopening the Edinburgh-Carlisle railway line as a private-enterprise venture.

After meeting the three directors of the Border Union Railway Company — Mr Robert Symes-Schutzmann, Mr Roy Perkins and Mr Martin Symms — Provost William Pate, Galashiels, said: "We were a little sceptical, but I must say these men are full of confidence and enthusiasm and determination. I think most of us came away convinced that something could be done."

The Duke of Roxburghe, convener of Roxburgh County Council, said: "The council tried very hard to stop British Rail closing the line in January, and I think anything that anyone can do to restore it is of benefit to the county." The council will decide at their next meeting whether to support the company.

It is already proposed to hold a meeting of local authorities from the Borders in the near future to consider the part the rail company could play in promoting tourism in the area. Provost Pate pointed out, however, that it would be difficult for local authorities to offer tangible help.

At a Press conference on Saturday, Mr Symms, managing director of a company which organises specialist holidays, stressed the tourist potential of the line; Mr Symes-Schutzmann, a BBC producer, pointed out the potential market from rail enthusiasts. Mr Perkins, a market research analyst, is organising a survey to assess the passenger and freight potential."

The *Scotsman* of 17th March 1969 gives prominent – and positive – coverage of BURCo's press launch two days earlier.
Courtesy of the Scotsman Publications Ltd

```
              In addition to purchasing the railway line, immediate
      capital will be needed for the provision of stock, workshop
      buildings and plant, the construction of a bridge over the
      railway for the M6 (Carlisle By-Pass), for the museum, and capital
      developments at Newcastleton. Thus the initial capital expenditure
      and profit and loss accounts will closely resemble those shown
      below:-
                            CAPITAL EXPENDITURE

                                                         £
      To-purchase of railway line, including resale
         of lifted track                               750,000
      To-purchase of locomotives & rolling stock
         including spares                               55,000
      To-Construction of Museum at Melrose              65,000
      To-capital injection at Newcastleton              30,000
      To-tunnel repair at Whitrope                      60,000
      To-bridge constructionat Harker                  170,000
      To-signal modifications at Carlisle               50,000
      To-workshops and plant at Riccarton              100,000
      To-timber handling equipment                      25,000
      To-signalling alterations for single line working 30,000
      To-new station construction                       40,000
      To-immediate working capital                     125,000


      TOTAL CAPITAL REQUIRED:                        1,500,000
```

This capital expenditure projection was one of just two financial tables in the 37-page *Border Union Railway Co. Ltd Feasibility Study* published by David Block Associates of London. The projected capital requirement of £1.5m is equivalent to £20m in today's prices.

David Spaven archive

```
                          REVENUE PER ANNUM
      Passenger:
                                                         £
              Passenger Traffic                     210-250,000
              Rail Tourist                          150-200,000
              Parcels (including wool prod.)         35- 37,000
             *Mails                                      ?

      Freight:
              Coal                                      10,000
              Timber                                    32,000
              Other                                    6-7,000
             *Pick-a-back                                 ?
      Rents & Property Incomes                          20,000
      Museum Income                                     12,000
      Miscellaneous (Films etc)                         10,000
                                                 _____
              TOTAL REVENUE                       485-578,000 plus

      * Revenue accruing from Royal Mails and Pick-a-back operations
      has not yet been estimated.

                         EXPENDITURE PER ANNUM
      Depreciation & Renewal Sinking Fund               65,000
      Amortisation                                      25,000
      Wages & Staff Charges                            105,000
      Fuels & Lubricants                                20,000
      Materials For Infrastruture                       80,000
      Materials for Rolling Stock                       16,000
      Admin. & General                                  10,000
      Miscellaneous                                      5,000
      Insurances                                        10,000
      Redundancy Payments                                  NIL
      Liscences                                          1,000
      Legal & Professional                               8,000
                                                       345,000
      Running Powers Charges                            75,000
      TOTAL EXPENDITURS                                420,000
      First  year operating surplus:-
                                          Revenue  £485-578,000
                                          Expenditure £ 420,000
                                                    £65 -158,000 +
```

The Profit & Loss page of BURCo's 1969 Feasibility Study report: fantasy economics? The large number of spelling errors in the report (there are three on this page alone) dismayed the Waverley Association and doubtless did little to convince potential backers of BURCo's professionalism.

David Spaven archive

Border Union Railway Co. Ltd.

Directors: R.M.G.Perkins,B.Sc.(Econ) Hons.
R.A.Symes-Schutzmann,Companion R.Ae.S.
M.C.H.Symms,B.A.Dip.Com.

Please Reply to:

BURCo's short-lived letterhead. At the foot of the full page was a registed office address at 52 High Holborn, London WC1. Both BURCo and the Waverley Association were very much London-centred, and although a majority of BURCo's 'associates' were Scotland-based, they were not brought into play effectively until late 1969, by which time the project was virtually doomed.

David Spaven archive

The only rail operation ever undertaken by BURCo: a flatbed container of logs is transferred from road to rail during a 3rd November 1969 demonstration at BR's Longtown freight depot.

Bruce McCartney

Track going, going, gone.

Looking south towards Riddings Junction, with the viaduct formerly carrying the Langholm branch over the Liddel Water trailing in from the right. The Up line here was lifted between January and March 1969, and the Down line on 3rd December 1970.

Oliver Hudson (courtesy of Rae Montgomery)

Birmingham Type 2 (aka Class 26) No. D5307, hauling a southbound inspection saloon, pauses in Hawick on 1st April 1970. The saloon was said to have been operated to allow scrap contractors to view the extent of track available for recovery, but it may – alternatively or additionally – have conveyed a portable Hallade Track Recorder, rumoured at the time to have been deployed by BR as part of a brief reconsideration of the railway's future as a timber carrier and diversionary route for the West Coast Main Line.

Bruce McCartney

D5307 and inspection saloon, heading south, emerge from the southern portal of Whitrope Tunnel on 1st April 1970. *Bruce McCartney*

Looking north towards Brunthill signal box, beyond which the connection to the RAF 14MU depot trails off to the left. This photo is thought to have been taken between August 1969 and August 1970, when only the Down line of the former Waverley Route between Brunthill and Longtown was still in operation. Today this is the location of Carlisle Warehousing's modern railhead, which has three sidings and has handled cement, steel and other rail traffics in recent years.

Bruce McCartney collection

The notice sunk in the former Up line of the Waverley Route near Lady Victoria Pit controlled the local operation of the first ever Scottish Railway Preservation Society tour on 23rd May 1970 (as well as local freight trains to the colliery until 1971). Between Millerhill and Lady Victoria, 'telephone and notice board' working was in operation, as it had been until 25th April 1969 on the section south to Hawick. *Allan McLean*

The Up line has gone, but virtually everything else remains intact at Shankend on 6th October 1970. The station building and signal box survive today in private ownership. *Norman Turnbull*

Railway navvies in modern incarnation: some 110 years after their predecessors had built the Waverley Route through Liddesdale, track recovery workers have the less heroic task of ripping up the railway at Three Bridges, near Scotch Dyke, in this shot thought to have been taken in late 1970, looking north.
Bruce McCartney collection

In its last years, Anglo-Scottish freight haulage over the Waverley Route was dominated by four types of traction: double-headed Clayton Type 1s, English Electric Type 3s, English Electric Type 4s and Brush Type 4s. Here one of the latter is involved in an altogether more mundane task, heading a southbound track recovery train near Scotch Dyke, probably in late 1970.
Bruce McCartney collection

The London Midland Region (LMR) section of the Waverley Route shrinks southwards near Scotch Dyke (between Riddings Junction and Longtown) in a photo likely to have been taken in late 1970. While Scottish Region lifted the Up line first, on various stretches south of Hawick, the LMR started with the Down line. Bruce McCartney believes this may have been to allow the recovery train to run straight through to Mossband Junction on the WCML; such was the track configuration, that if the train had been on the Down line this would have necessitated additional shunting at the Longtown level crossing in order to gain access to the Mossband branch. *Bruce McCartney collection*

A view south towards rakes of track recovery wagons on the Down main and Down refuge siding at Newcastleton. These are the level crossing gates where dramatic scenes were enacted around the last passenger train on 5th / 6th January 1969. The Up line here was lifted between January and March 1969, and the Down line in late December 1970. *Oliver Hudson (courtesy of Rae Montgomery)*

On 1st January 1971, Borthwick Bank signal box is a sorry sight, in this northbound view showing both tracks of the Waverley Route still in situ. The box had closed in July 1968, leaving an eight-mile block section between Heriot and Lady Victoria Pit boxes. *Rae Montgomery*

The utiltarian box at Riccarton South overlooks the remaining Down line and Down loop shortly before the last tracks were lifted here in late January / early February 1971. The former Border Counties line to Hexham, trailing off to the left, had closed to passengers in 1956 and freight in 1958.
Oliver Hudson (courtesy of Rae Montgomery)

The old Border Counties bay platform lies abandoned at Riccarton Junction, shortly before the last tracks were lifted here in late January / early February 1971. The station building housed a Co-operative store until 1965. *Oliver Hudson (courtesy of Rae Montgomery)*

A track recovery train hauled by a Class 08 shunter creeps northwards along the Slitrig Water Valley between Shankend and Stobs, not long before the remaining Down line was lifted in March 1971.
Oliver Hudson (courtesy of Rae Montgomery)

This view looking south at Shankend was taken not long after the last track (the Down line) was lifted here in February 1971. *Oliver Hudson (courtesy of Rae Montgomery)*

No longer disturbed by trains, a ewe and lamb relax by the former Down line at Shankend, some time after both tracks were lifted here in February 1971. *Rae Montgomery*

English Electric Type 4 (aka Class 40) No. D286 inches a northbound track recovery train across Heriot level crossing on 21st March 1971, the train crew having earlier struggled to clear the crossing gates of accumulated snow previously ploughed off the road.   *KM Falconer*

The double track railway has shrunk back to the Teviot Viaduct in Hawick in this view taken from the cab of a Class 08 shunting loco on track recovery work, thought to be in early April 1971.
Bruce McCartney

Thought to have been taken on 18th April 1971 – the day the last track was lifted from the Teviot Viaduct – this must have been a grim sight for the photographer, Gordon Hall, who had been the last signalman at Hawick on the night of 5th / 6th January 1969. *Gordon Hall*

Like the previous photo, this was taken from the vantage point of a telegraph pole, but looking north at the weed-infested railway corridor, just days before all the track was lifted in late April 1971.
Gordon Hall

In the spring of 1971, two years after the last freight train had departed, much of the physical infrastructure of the railway – including a road-served parcels and sundries depot – remained intact at Galashiels station. Today the scene is almost unrecognisable, with only the metal gates and two stone columns (plus a further two off-camera to the right) surviving as the last evidence that there was once a railway station here. *David Spaven*

A Class 08 heading north through Belses station with a track recovery train, thought to be during the period between the lifting of both tracks south of Belses on 29th May 1971 and north of Belses on 7th June 1971. *Oliver Hudson, courtesy of Rae Montgomery*

Kelso Junction photographed from a track recovery train (with another on the Down line in the middle distance), possibly in the summer of 1971. The Kelso branch closed to passengers in 1964 and to freight in 1968, and latterly had only a single-lead connection to the Up line of the Waverley Route.
Oliver Hudson (courtesy of Rae Montgomery)

In late March 1971, this was the photographer's last ever journey on the Waverley Route, in the cab of a Clayton Type 1 approaching St Boswells with a northbound track recovery train. Above the engine's bonnet can be glimpsed the tower of the headquarters of Roxburgh County Council, strategically sited in Newtown St Boswells to avoid exacerbating rivalry between the county's main towns of Hawick, Jedburgh, Kelso and Melrose, and – ironically – due to its rail connectivity.
Bruce McCartney

Smashed windows and weeds – prior to complete bulldozing of the site – are the sad fate of St Boswells station in this view looking north in summer 1971.
Oliver Hudson (courtesy of Rae Montgomery)

A Class 08 hauls a track recovery train north through St Boswells, some time between the completion of lifting both lines just north of Belses on 7th June 1971 and at Melrose on 16th September 1971.
Oliver Hudson (courtesy of Rae Montgomery)

Stacks of recovered track panels and track recovery wagons accumulate at St Boswells in summer 1971 in this view looking north, with the former goods shed to the right.
Oliver Hudson (courtesy of Rae Montgomery)

A track recovery crane hard at work at St Boswells on 17th May 1971, with one of the Eildon Hills just visible to the north.
Norman Turnbull

A coal train hauled by a Clayton Type 1 shunts beside the closed Lady Victoria Pit signal box in 1971, with an enormous stockpile of coal at Newbattle Coal Preparation Plant behind. Rail services ceased at 'Lady Vic' in December of that year, and at Butlerfield in June 1972. *Bill Roberton*

Believed to date from summer 1971, this view looking south from Galashiels station shows on the left the former engine shed and one of the single-aspect colour-light signals installed by the LNER in its 1937 Gala area resignalling project. *Oliver Hudson (courtesy of Rae Montgomery)*

Looking south from Galashiels station, almost certainly in autumn 1971. By 8th November 1971, lifting of all tracks had reached as far north as Bowshank Tunnel, between Gala and Stow. An NCL (National Carriers Ltd) lorry lurks on the right, NCL having been set up under the 1968 Transport Act to handle parcels and sundries, including collections to, and deliveries from, railway stations. *Oliver Hudson (courtesy of Rae Montgomery)*

A Class 08 eases a northbound track recovery train over the level crossing at Heriot on 10th September 1971. *Norman Turnbull*

Taken from the station footbridge, this view south at Fountainhall shows a Class 08-hauled track recovery train heading north on Sunday 12th September 1971. *Norman Turnbull*

A Class 08 hauls a track recovery train north over one of the distinctive bowstring plate-girder bridge or 'upturned fish belly' bridges crossing the Gala Water, in the vicinity of Fountainhall, on Sunday 12th September 1971. These bridges have survived to grace the modern Borders Railway, albeit with their clean lines somewhat marred by the inevitable safety fencing. *Norman Turnbull*

On 3rd October 1971, just north of Tynehead, a train of track panels hauled by a Class 08 is nearing its destination at a temporary track recovery base at Borthwick Bank. *Norman Turnbull*

Class 08 diesel No. D3889 in charge of a track recovery train just north of Galashiels station on 14th October 1971. Driver J Patillo of Hawick is 'retired but back in harness'.

George Kinghorn (courtesy of Dougie Squance and Bruce McCartney)

Two and a half years without tracks had elapsed by the time this photo of Stow station was taken, looking north on 19th June 1974. Due to the determined efforts of local campaigners nearly 30 years later, the initial Borders Railway plan to omit any station stop at Stow was over-turned, and a subsequent official proposal to demolish the building and replace it with a bus shelter was also defeated. Stow is one of just two Borders Railway stations with surviving 1849 buildings, the other being Gorebridge. *Norman Turnbull*

The vast area of redundant railway land in central Galashiels – and its potential for industrial and retail development – can readily be appreciated from this 5th April 1975 view, taken looking north west from the southern end of the former freight depot. Ironically, at this very time BR and the new Borders Regional Council were seriously discussing the feasibility of reinstating a passenger rail service from Edinburgh to Galashiels or St Boswells. *Bill Roberton*

The overgrown solum and platforms at Melrose make for a sorry sight in this eastward-looking view on 5th June 1975. Despite the arrival of the new A6091 Melrose bypass here 13 years later, the Up platform and station building survive today, in the latter case as an A-listed structure.
Bill Roberton

13 years later, the former Down platform and building had sadly disappeared under the A6091 Melrose bypass, but happily the urinal in the foreground survives today as a working facility at Bridgenorth on the Severn Valley Railway!
Bill Roberton

Lingering signs of the former railway, looking north at Hawick's platforms on 5th June 1975. Just three months later even these vestiges would disappear, when the Teviot Viaduct was demolished and the station site cleared for the construction of a leisure centre. *Bill Roberton*

Nine years and one day since closure, and the adjacent forest growth is transforming its surroundings, but Riccarton Junction station is still immediately recognisable on 7th January 1978 – with its surviving footbridge and telephone box – albeit in a sorry condition prior to eventual demolition. The lost Waverley Route was now settling into a long period where the solum gradually returned to nature, its 107 year history as an Anglo-Scottish main line increasingly – but never entirely – forgotten. *Alan Young*

CHAPTER 4

Forty-three years later…

ONCE the last track panel of the 87 route miles between Millerhill Junction and the Brunthill RAF depot in Carlisle had been lifted in 1972, the lost Waverley Route settled into a long period where the solum gradually returned to nature. A few stretches were used for burying utilities and there were intermittent breaches for road construction, and – even more crassly – house building.

As the author recounts in detail in *Waverley Route: the battle for the Borders Railway*, after more than two decades in the wilderness the still-pressing need for a Borders railway eventually rose to the top of the political agenda. But the official rail re-opening project, which began in 1999 – led initially by Scottish Borders Council and then Transport Scotland – could only have happened with, first, the foresight of Simon Longland and the Borders Transport Futures company in the mid-1990s, and, second, the determination of the grassroots movement led by the Campaign for Borders Rail in the late 1990s and early 2000s, supported by the innovative ideas of the Waverley Route Trust later in the latter decade.

It was a very long slog for campaigners, but there was joy when the Borders Railway finally opened to Gala and Tweedbank in 2015. Unfortunately, due to the Scottish Government's ludicrously pessimistic passenger forecasts for the Borders stations (equating to two passengers per train at Gala and at Tweedbank, compared to an actual nine and 15 respectively in the first year of operation), the line's infrastructure is seriously sub-optimal. With just nine and a half miles of double-track (compared to a planned 16 miles) on the $30\frac{1}{2}$ mile new railway, reliability is fragile and there is no spare capacity for any trains other than the regular ScotRail service – except in the evenings and on Sundays.

But the railway is once again a key part of the Borders economy and society. No more is the region the only one in Britain without a train service, and no longer are Gala and Hawick further from the rail network than any other towns of their size in Britain. And part of the BURCo vision has at long last been realised, with just over a third of the Waverley Route back in action.

The Campaign for Borders Rail is now pushing hard for railway extension southwards from Tweedbank to Hawick (in particular, as it has suffered more from the loss of the Waverley Route than any other Borders town) and onwards to Carlisle. South of Hawick, several major railway structures have gone, and – critically – the rail corridor traverses largely unpopulated countryside. Indeed, even the Victorians had their doubts about the viability of constructing a railway through the 'Debatable Land' by Riccarton and Newcastleton.

For the author, the prospects south of Hawick hinge fundamentally on the potential for timber being moved by rail from the Kielder, Wauchope, Newcastleton and Kershope Forests, as identified by Borders Transport Futures in the mid-1990s – based on the railway being re-opened as a single-track route up to Riccarton from the current Ministry of Defence Longtown branch, with a branch onwards to Kielder. This then would leave 'just' 13 miles of empty, traffic-less country to connect with a Hawick-Tweedbank-Edinburgh passenger railway.

Perhaps we may yet see trains again in Liddesdale, the vision which so inspired Roy Perkins and his Border Union dream back in 1969.

Not even the most optimistic scenario for the return of trains to Liddesdale would resurrect a station here. Riddings Junction station closed in 1964 when the Langholm branch passenger services were withdrawn. This shot of the Up side station building – thought to have been taken in Spring 1969 or 1970 – shows both Up and Down tracks in situ. Many of the station structures on the railway south of Hawick were not typical of North British Railway designs, and the brick construction at Riddings may have been due to the presence of a nearby brick works.

Oliver Hudson (courtesy of Rae Montgomery)

APPENDIX 1

BR freight working timetable 1968-69

Down services (Carlisle-Edinburgh)

M Cns	Head Code	5S09	4S40	4S41	4S43	3S05*	4S42	8S50	3S05*	4K	3S49*	4S46
	Train description					01.00 Garston to B'gate Upper			11.48 Ford Sdgs to B'gate Upper		15.15 King's Norton to B'gateUr	
	Restrictions / notes		Limited Load	Limited Load		Suspended	Limited Load	Limited Load	Suspended	Assured Arrival Service		Limited Load
	Days of operation	MX	MX	M–S	M–S	WFO	M–S	SX	SO	SX	TTHSO	SO
	Reporting point											
0 00	Carlisle Canal Jct dep	23.45	01.15	04.50	05.55	07.55	08.30	13.25				21.30
	CARLISLE NEW YARD dep	23.54	01.23	04.58	06.04		08.38	13.34				21.35
	Stainton Jct arr	00.04	01.33	05.08	06.14		08.48	13.44				21.50
	dep								17.50		20.57	
	Brunthill	00.11	01.39	05.14	06.21	08.00	08.54	13.52				21.56
22 64	Longtown Jct	00.22	01.48	05.23	06.32	08.09	09.03	14.06	18.02		21.06	22.05
30 73	Newcastleton	00.48	02.12	05.47	06.55	08.32	09.27	14.38	18.28		21.09	22.29
43 74	Riccarton	01.10	02.33	06.08	07.20	08.51	09.48	15.00	18.49		21.32	22.50
	HAWICK arr										21.51	
	dep	01.33	02.55	06.30	07.43	09.13	10.10	15.25	19.11	19.40	22.13	23.12
56 16	St. Boswells arr									20.02	22.29	
	dep	01.52	03.13	06.48	08.02	09.29	10.28	15.48	19.31	20.14		23.30
63 18	Galashiels arr							16.01		20.40		
	dep	02.02	03.23	06.58	08.12	09.37	10.38	16.11	19.38	21.07	22.37	23.40
77 52	Heriot	02.27	03.42	07.17	08.37	10.01	10.57	16.41	20.02	21.25	23.01	23.59
88 40	Hardengreen Jct	02.45	03.57	07.32	08.55	10.17	11.12	17.01	20.18		23.24	00.14
	MILLERHILL YARD											
91 14	North Down Reception arr	02.53	04.07	07.42	09.03	10.29	11.22	17.09	21.30	21.33	23.35	00.24
92 75	Down Yard Departure arr											

Notes: Bold times indicate train calls at this point; light times indicate train passes this point.
*Air-Braked private company block load train.
Heavy black line under Head Code denotes NFTP booked service.

137

Up services (Edinburgh-Carlisle)

Head Code	4M46	4M49	6	6	4M60	4M65	3M45*	3M52*	8M51	4M80	4M56
Train description							01.00 B'gate Ur to King's Norton	14.45 B'gate Ur to Ford Sdgs MWO Garston FO			To Oldham
Restrictions / notes		Limited Load			Limited Load	Limited Load		Suspended	Limited Load	Limited Load	Limited Load
Days of operation	M-S	M-S	SO	SX	M-S	SX	MWFO	MWFO	SX	SX	SX
Reporting point (M Chs)											
0 00 MILLERHILL UP YARD dep	**01.25**	**02.25**	**03.15**	**03.15**	**05.00**	**09.52**	**12.53**	**16.00**	**16.45**	**20.10**	**21.30**
02 56 Hardengreen Jct	01.32	02.32	03.24		05.07	09.59	13.00	16.07	16.54	20.17	21.37
13 44 Heriot	01.59	02.59	03.52		05.34	10.26	13.25	16.32	17.23	20.45	22.04
22 78 Galashiels arr				04.14D					17.48		
dep	02.20	03.20	04.12	04.24	05.55	10.47	13.42	16.49	17.58	21.05	22.25
22 64 St. Boswells arr				04.36							
35 00 dep	02.29	03.29	04.22	04.56	06.04	10.56	13.51	16.58	18.13	21.14	22.34
47 22 HAWICK arr			**04.42**						**18.36**		
dep	02.47	03.47			06.22	11.14	14.06	17.13	**18.51**	21.32	22.52
60 23 Riccarton	03.17	04.17			06.52	11.44	14.35	17.42	19.27	22.02	23.22
68 32 Newcastleton	03.28	04.28			07.03	11.55	14.45	17.52	19.41	22.13	23.33
83 04 Longtown Jct	03.55	04.55			07.25	12.17	15.04	18.11	20.09	22.40	23.55
86 33 Mossband	04.02	05.02			07.32	12.24	15.11	18.18	20.19	22.47	00.02
89 46 CARLISLE NEW YARD arr	**04.10**	**05.10**			**07.40**	**12.35**	**15.22**	**18.29**	**20.28**	**22.55**	**00.13**

Notes: Bold times indicate train calls at this point; light times indicate train passes this point.
*Air-braked private company block load train.
Heavy black line under Head Code denotes NFTP booked service.
D after train arrival time indicates train stops only to detach.

[Transcribed from BR Scottish Region Section E Working Timetable of Freight Trains Ref B.R. 31099/5]

[D Spaven archive]

APPENDIX 2

Andrew Boyd's notes of Trip E10, Millerhill-Hawick, 24th March 1969

Trip planned today – to Hawick by train (the daily trip freight, 9am Millerhill-Hawick), with Bruce [McCartney] and Eric Glendinning.

Our train left Millerhill Yard at about 09.00. Our train, hauled by D7608, consisted of about 23 wagons + 1 brake van. It ran as class '6' (the loco display headboard showed class '8'). We travelled on the b/van as far as Fountainhall; for the section to St Boswells we travelled on the loco; and covered the final section in the brake-van.

We were stopped at Lady Victoria box for several minutes (giving a chance to watch the colliery pugs shunting), before getting the road. I noted that many signal arms had been taken down (eg those for the now-closed Hardengreen Junction), but several distants survived as fixed distants – eg approaching the L.C's; near Hawick North; etc..

The train crew opened and shut the gates at Heriot L.C., and again at Fountainhall – so, despite some fast running (we touched 45-50[1]), it was about 10.35 am when we reached Galashiels. On arrival, those wagons for St Boswells and Hawick were left in the up station platform, and the rest of our train reversed on to the down line, and then ran into the goods yard to drop off wagons for Gala (we had about 9 or 10 – mostly coal, but there were 3 Esso tank wagons), shunt the yard, and pick up freight for Millerhill (freight and empty wagons ex-Gala and St Boswells are taken on to Hawick, so that the freight train can run nonstop back to Millerhill).

Our work at Galashiels took rather a long time, so it was about 11.55 when we set off (having taken about 2 or so wagons ex-Galashiels) from Gala for St Boswells. We then stopped at St Boswells; the "for-Hawick" portion was left on the up line, and the wagons for St Boswells + the wagons ex-Gala (I think there was only one wagon for St Boswells) were shunted into the yard. This again took a long time; eventually we were off again, having taken on 15 wagons, mostly timber for Devonport, but including two potato vans, one for Darlington, the other for Basingstoke.

So we now had about 28 wagons on (all our wagons for Hawick carried coal from the Northumberland / Durham area – eg from Shilbottle and

Derwenthaugh collieries).

(Note: a travelling signalman, who joined at Gala, worked the points from the otherwise closed Galashiels and St Boswells signal boxes.[2])

I noted that, south of Gorebridge, virtually all of the station and signal box nameboards etc had been removed.

Maintaining about 30-40-45-50 mph through Belses & Hassendean, we came to a stop in Hawick Up platform (ie passenger station), 1.35pm to 1.40pm. The loco then left the Gala and St Boswells section in the station, after running round the train, and prepared to start to shunt the yard (which contained only a handful of wagons; note there was no Clayton around – track-lifting south of Hawick has stopped; we then left the station.

Bruce and myself shortly afterwards returned by car to Edinburgh along the A7. We stopped off at Burnfoot, and watched D7608 return northwards on the down line (both up and down lines are still in use), with 23 wagons + brakevan (the wagons included a bogie bolster, loaded with timber). The time we saw it passing was about 2.45pm (Burnfoot is the housing scheme on the north side of Hawick).

So ended what may (or may not) be my last trip on the Waverley Route.

1: The BR Scottish Region General Instructions and Notices (Reference No. 7D) noted that the maximum permissible speed from Hawick South Ground Frame (ie the old signal box) to Millerhill was 45mph, with a few lower speed restrictions at specific locations (courtesy of Andrew Boyd).

2: Reference to Hawick South box was omitted, Andrew commenting in 2018: 'Please bear in mind that on the day I would have scribbled notes on scraps of paper and then written these up in my note-book when I got home, probably the same evening, sometimes reliant on my memory when the notes were unclear or incomplete . . . I should have been more careful and attentive, but I did not realise that these notes would be published half a century later.'! We should indeed be very grateful to Andrew for his foresight in making, and archiving, this detailed record of a brief, but fascinating, moment in Scottish railway history.

BIBLIOGRAPHY AND SOURCES

David Block Associates, *Border Union Railway Co. Ltd Feasibility Study* (privately published, 1969)

Mullay, AJ. *Rails across the Border* (Patrick Stephens, 1990)

Mullay, AJ. *Scottish Region: A History* 1948-1973 (Tempus, 2006)

Robotham, R. *The Waverley Route: The Postwar Years* (Ian Allan, 1999)

Spaven, DL. *Waverley Route: the life, death and rebirth of the Borders Railway* (Argyll Publishing, 2012)

Spaven, DL. *Waverley Route: the battle for the Borders Railway* (Third Edition, Stenlake Publishing, 2017)

Thomas, J (revised by Alan JS Paterson). *A Regional History of the Railways of Great Britain, Volume 6 Scotland: The Lowlands and the Borders* (David & Charles, 1984)

White, HP. *Forgotten Railways* (David & Charles, 1986).

Websites

www.disused-stations.org.uk

Public archive sources:

The undernoted files are held by the **National Records of Scotland** in Edinburgh (reference DD for the Scottish Office Development Department; SEP for the Scottish Economic Planning Council).

DD17/1478 (1968-70)

SEP16/58 (1968-69).

The undernoted files are held by the **National Archives** in London (Kew):

AN169/108: 1969-70 BR correspondence with Border Union Railway Company.

Private archive sources:

Andrew Boyd

Ian Holoran

Bruce McCartney

Rae Montgomery

The late Roy Perkins

David and the late Frank Spaven.

INDEX

A *Regional History of the Railways of Great Britain Volume 6, Scotland: The Lowlands and Borders*, 9
A4 Pacific, 29
A6091 road, 13, 16, 101, 102, 133
A68 road, 102
A7 road, 43, 48, 63, 102, 140
A74 road, 50, 51, 77
Abbott, Stan, 88
Aberdeen, 45
Accrington, 45
Anglo-Scottish railway, 9, 10, 39
April fool, 103
Argo Transacord, 93
Army Railway Warrant, 74
Arnton Fell, 37
Austrian railway system, 52
Aviemore, 46

B6318 road, 95
B6399 road, 90
Ballast trains, 44
Bank of Scotland, 47
Bardney, 64
Barnes, RA, 67, 70
Basic Railway, 53
Basingstoke, 139
BBC, 35, 78, 108
Beattock, 44
Beeching Report, 5, 9, 53, 64, 105
Bell, Ian, 104
Belses, 32, 124, 126, 140
Berwickshire County Council, 46
Birmingham Type 2, 39, 102, 103, 108, 113
Block post, 20, 37, 38
Block, David, 80
Blue Peter, 73
Bluebell Railway, 42
Bo'ness and Kinneil Railway, 46, 108, 109
Boat of Garten, 46
Bonham-Carter, Mark, 42, 74
Border Counties Railway, 63, 119
Border Economic Planning Group, 47
Border TV, 59
Borders Consultative Group, 62
Borders expatriates, 45
Borders Railway, 6, 16, 23, 24, 25, 28, 59, 105, 130, 132, 135
Borders Railway, first passenger train, 14
Borders Regional Council, 132
Borders tourism, 40, 60
Borders Transport Futures, 135, 136
Borders, only region without rail services, 10, 109, 135
Borthwick Bank, 108, 117, 131
Bovis Holmes, 42
Bowland, 48
Bowshank Tunnel, 16, 17, 129
Boyd, Andrew, 7, 12, 39, 40, 48, 58, 139
BR Annual Report, 41
BR freight working, 7
BR track-lifting diagram, 6
BR Type 2 , 12, 16, 40
Branch line services, 27, 30, 31
Bridge 13, 8
Bridge 22, 22
Bridge 23, 22
Bridge 97, 25
Bridge 197, 89
Bridge 204, 91
Bridge 205, 91
Bridge 243, 95
Bridge 244, 96
Bridge 253, 99
Bridge 254, 94
Bridgenorth, 133

Britannia class, 98
British Rail, 5, 7, 8, 10, 14, 26, 36, 37, 41, 43, 44, 46, 50, 51, 53, 55, 57, 59, 61, 63, 64, 65, 68, 71, 73, 79, 81, 83, 84, 87, 88, 95, 103, 105, 106; Eastern Region, 53; Estate Surveyor, 65; Modernisation Plan (1955), 48; ban on main-line steam, 35, 49; concern over liabilities, 77, 78; infrastructure economies, 26, 37, 50; interest charges, 71, 73, 76; London Midland Region, 38, 52, 58, 65, 87, 107, 109, 117; longest signalling block section, 38; parcels service to Galashiels, 49; Property Board, 77, 78; Scottish Region, 38, 58, 65, 66, 70, 76, 80, 83, 87, 109, 117; track diagram, 43, 70, 108
British Railways Board, 42, 47, 49, 50, 51, 53, 57, 58, 66, 67, 69, 70, 71, 72, 73, 74, 75, 76, 78, 80, 87, 109; Estate Manager, 56, 58; Press Office Brief (1969), 76
Brush Type 4, 39, 116
Bullhead panels, 44
BURCo – British Rail negotiations, 44, 47, 49, 51, 58, 65, 66, 69, 70, 74, 75, 76, 79, 83, 87, 89
BURCo – Waverley Association relationship, 6, 43, 54, 61, 67, 73, 74
BURCo associates, 43, 52, 70, 71, 76, 78, 80
BURCo directors, 45, 47, 54, 56, 61, 67, 69, 70, 71, 73, 76, 78, 79, 84, 109
BURCo projected staff numbers, 54
BURCo proposed fares, 57
BURCo provisional timetable, 57
BURCo rolling stock, 51, 53
BURCo shares, 47
BURCo survey, 48
BURCo, headquarters, 60
BURCo, letterhead, 112
Burmah Oil, 75, 76, 77, 86
Burnfoot, 140
Bus services, 10, 34, 35, 43

Campaign for Borders Rail, 54, 87, 135
Carlisle, 5, 6, 10, 27, 36, 39, 43, 49, 51, 52, 53, 57, 66, 88, 103, 105, 108, 135, 136; bypass, 50, 51; Canal Junction, 20, 105; Canal station, 69; Citadel, 49, 69; No.3 signal box, 69
Carlisle – Glasgow line (via Kilmarnock), 104
Carlisle Warehousing, 105, 114
Carlisle/Longtown/Mossband triangle, 7
Carnforth, 108
Castrol House, 76
Cental Belt of Scotland, 107
Church of Scotland, 10
Churchillian Wisdom, 11
Clarke, Alan, 76
Class 5, 45
Class 08 shunter, 108, 120, 122, 124, 126, 131, 130, 131
Class 17, 38
Class 25, 12, 16, 40
Class 26, 39, 108, 113
Class 37, 11, 15, 39, 108
Class 40, 108, 122
Class 45, 108
Class 46, 108
Class 47, 39, 108
Class 57, 108
Clayton Type-1, 11, 17, 38, 39, 44, 48, 108, 118, 125, 127, 140
Coal traffic, 17, 19, 27, 37, 38, 40, 64, 97, 109, 127, 139
Coleman, Ralph, 39

Commonwealth Games (1970), 63
Concrete sleepers, 44, 99
Continuously-welded rail, 108
Countryside Commission for Scotland, 107
County Clerk of Roxburgh, 42
Crewe, 69
Cribbin, John, 61
Cumbrian Railways Association, 6

Dalry – Kilmarnock line, 104
Darlington, 139
Darnick Siding, 10
Dart Valley Railway, 62
David Block Associates, 59, 11
Dawson, Garth, 45
Debatable Land, 136
Derby lightweight unit, 52, 53
Derwenthaugh Colliery, 140
Devonport, 139
Diesel Multiple Units, 41, 51, 52, 53, 57
Direct Rail Services, 108
Disused Railway Lines in Scotland: a Strategic Appraisal, 107
Disused Stations website, 7, 32
Donations to BURCo, 45
Double-track railway, 13, 19, 22, 37, 41, 59, 84, 104, 118
Douglas, Jimmy, 10
Downing Street 10, 10, 55
Draft Report, 40, 41, 42, 61, 69
Duncan, Mr, 65
Dynamic loop, 13

Ealing Commedy, 35
Earl of Dalkeith, 10, 55
East Coast Main Line, 55
Eastern Border Development Association, 46
Edinburgh, 5, 6, 22, 39, 43, 44, 46, 57, 59, 63, 66, 68, 74, 75, 81, 84, 88, 102, 103, 104, 105, 108, 132; Waverley, 49, 55, 66
Edinburgh City Bypass, 46
Edinburgh Evening News, 61
Edinburgh University Railway Society, 39
Edinburgh University Report, 57
Edinburgh-Hawick Railway, 8, 9, 88
Edinburgh-St Pancras sleeper, 10
Eildon Hills, 13, 127
Electric locomotives, 52
Electrification, 52
Ellesmere Port , 63
Elliot, Madge, 10, 47, 55, 59
Engineering traffic, 44
English Electric Type 3, 11, 15, 39, 116
English Electric type 4, 108, 116, 118, 122
Eskbank & Dalkeith, 8, 20
Excursion traffic, 36, 63

Fairmont Railway Motors Incorporated, 52
Falahill Summit, 38, 40
Feasibility Study, 40, 41, 51, 53, 57, 59-61, 62, 63, 65, 66, 68, 69, 70, 74, 84, 111; ; Burmah Oil new study, 75, 77; need for an independent study, 71, 79, 81; presentation errors, 60, 61, 111
Ffestiniog Railway, 62
Fiennes, Gerry, 53, 55, 56, 62, 63
Filming contracts, 59, 60
Final revenue-earning train, 17, 49
Flat bottomed track, 44, 99
Fleetwood-Shaw, John, 52
Flood, 1948, 30
Flying Scotsman Enterprises, 35
Forestry Commission, 60, 63, 64
Forgotten Railways, 10
Former rail travellers, 34

Former railway solum, 16, 101, 102, 105, 133, 134
Forrest, Norris, 45
Fountainhall, 23, 24, 130, 139; exchange sidings, 23; goods yard, 23; level crossing, 37, 48; signal box, 37, 55
Freight only railway, 5, 39
Freight services, 6, 14, 19, 105, 130

Gala Water, 16, 23, 25
Galashiels, 6, 10, 11, 14, 15, 25, 26, 27, 28, 29, 31, 37, 38, 46, 52, 55, 57, 59, 65, 82, 101, 107, 124, 127, 128, 129, 131, 132, 135, 139, 140; British Railways Parcels service, 49, 124; engine shed, 28, 29; freight depot, 27; freight sidings, 8, 37, 48, 55; goods offices, 28; parcels clerk, 39; signal box, 17, 26, 37, 49; waiting shelter, 27
General Election, 1970, 81, 102
General freight traffic, 17, 38, 40, 60, 64, 97
Glasgow, 44, 65, 75
Glendinning, Eric, 40, 139
Golden Bridge, 90
Golding, Chris, 89
Gore Glen, 22
Gorebridge, 22, 23, 57, 132, 140; station building, 23
Government, 7, 36, 47, 81, 82, 87, 101, 102
Government subsidy, 62, 84, 85
Grainger, Thomas, 20
Grant, John, 42, 43, 86
Grapes Hotel, 37
Greenlaw, 30
Ground frame retention, 37, 38, 49

Hall, Gordon, 10, 123
Hallade Track Recorder, 103, 104, 113
Hammond, Roy, 66, 71, 73, 75, 77, 78, 79
Handford, Peter, 93
Hardengreen Junction, 20, 139
Hardengreen, signal box, 37
Harker, 96
Harper, Ken, 6
Harvey, Mr, 65
Harvey, RC 'Reg', 48
Hassendean, 140
Hawick, 5, 7, 8, 10, 12, 14, 15, 17, 27, 32, 33, 34, 36, 37, 38, 39, 40, 41, 44, 47, 48, 52, 54, 55, 56, 57, 59, 62, 64, 65, 71, 82, 84, 88, 89, 90, 101, 102, 104, 108, 113, 115, 119, 122, 123, 134, 135, 136, 139, 140; Carlisle bound platform, 10; coal sidings, 14; freight depot, 14, 34, 48; gasworks, 32; leisure centre, 14, 34, 134; North Signal Box, 33, 139; South Signal Box, 10, 33, 37, 38, 39, 44, 49
Hawick Burgh Council, 65
Hawick News, 59, 72, 106
Hawick Town Council, 48
Hawick Train Register, 72
Hawick-Newcastleton bus service, sabotage, 35
Headquarters Scotland (Army), 74
Hellifield, 88
Henshaw, David, 44
Herbert, HM, 66, 72, 73, 139
Heriot, 37, 108, 118, 129; signal box, 37, 55, 117
Hexham, 63, 119
Hi-Rail equipment, 52
Hinchcliffe, Mr G, 35
Hollingsworth, Brian, 36
Holoran, Christine, 5, 48
Holoran, Ian, 5, 8, 35, 43, 45, 46, 48, 56, 79, 80, 81, 86

Hope, J, 38
House of Commons, 35
Hovertrain, 77
Howard, Major, 74
Howieson, JM, 82
Hudson, Oliver, 6
Hughes, John, 75, 77
Huntie gouk, 103

I tried to run a railway, 53
I.C.I, 107
Inspection saloon, 102, 104, 113, 114
Isle of Man, 36
Isle of Man, narrow gauge network, 36

Jamieson, Bill, 6
Journey times, 57

Kelso, 46, 47, 125
Kelso Junction, 31, 125
Kensington, 70
Kent & East Sussex Railway, 42
Kershope Burn, 95
Kershope Forest, 63, 136
Kershope, signal box, 38, 95
Keswick branch, 53
Kielder Forest, 63, 136
Kincardine power station, 109
Kingmoor Yard, 49, 105
Kyle, James, 42

Lady Victoria Colliery, 19, 46, 107, 109; sidings, 15
Lady Victoria Pit, signal box, 18, 20, 21, 22, 38, 44, 48, 49, 55, 66, 80, 109, 115, 117, 129, 139
Lake District, 59
Lamb, Bernard, 7, 53, 105
Langholm branch, 113
Lauder Light Railway, 23, 46
Lawrence, RLE, 58
Lazard Brothers, 88
Leeds, 88
Leith Docks, 64
Leyland Gas Turbines, 107
Liddel Viaduct, 94, 113
Liddesdale, 6, 35, 116, 136
Light Railway Act (1896), 58
Light Railway Order, 58, 66, 73
Lincolnshire, 64
Liverpool Docks, 64
Llangollen Railway, 39
London, 27, 35, 37, 49, 53, 71, 76, 109
London and North Eastern Railway, 26, 130
London Midland Region, British Rail, 38, 52, 58, 65, 87, 107, 109, 117
Longland, Simon, 135
Longtown, 5, 6, 7, 10, 36, 51, 55, 66, 76, 80, 84, 96, 98, 99, 104, 105, 109, 114, 119, 136; freight depot, 63, 96, 97, 105; freight traffic, 51; water tower, 98
Longtown – Carlisle line, 50, 51
Longtown – Gretna line, 51
Longtown – Mossband Junction line, 50
Lord Ailsa, 36
Lord Melgund, 43, 69, 70, 71, 72, 74, 75, 77, 78, 79, 106
Lostock Motive Power Depot, 45
Lycett, Michael, 43, 70, 71
Lyneside , 100; signal box, 100, 105

M6 road, 63, 64, 105
Maben, Rev Brydon, 10, 54, 55; arrest, 10
Mabon, Dickson, 101, 102
MacIntosh, Iain, 6

Main line, 20, 37
Main-line steam, 35, 36
Mansfield Road, 34
Marsh, Richard, 9, 40, 47, 49, 88, 101
Mary Celeste, 5, 30
Masterton, David, 48
Mathieson, J, 43
McBain, James, 38
McCartney, Bruce, 6, 7, 40, 48, 60, 82, 102, 104, 117, 139, 140
McGuinness, JH, 82, 102
McLean, Allan, 44, 104
McMichael, Hugh, 43, 71, 72, 74, 75, 76, 77
McNaughton, Lt. Col., 56
Melbury House, 49
Melrose, 16, 57, 60, 101, 126, 133; bypass, 13, 13, 133; proposed railway museum, 60; urinal, 133
Merseyside, 6
Merseyside Transport, 57
Miles Beevor, 29
Miller, John, 20
Millerhill, 8, 12, 13, 15, 17, 20, 21, 38, 39, 44, 46, 48, 49, 72, 105, 109, 115, 135, 139
Millerhill Yard, 7, 19, 37, 55, 109
Millerhill-Kingmoor working, 39
Minister of Transport, 9, 47, 49, 58, 83, 103
Ministry of Transport, 56, 77, 82, 101
Minnesota, 52
Modern Railways, 103, 104
Monorail, 77
Montgomery, Rae, 64, 76, 104, 107, 109
Mossband Junction, 50, 105, 117
Mullay, Alexander, 9, 57, 80, 109
Multi-fuel pipeline, proposal, 75, 77
Murray, Albert, 101, 102
Murrayfield Stadium, 48

National Archives, Richmond (Kew), 7, 53, 79, 87, 105
National Carriers Limited, 129
National Commercial & Glyns, 56
National Farmers Union, 78
National Records of Scotland, 7, 64, 76, 107, 109
National Union of Railworkers, 43, 54
Need for a robust business study, 46
Network Rail, 22
New road construction, 101
Newbattle Coal Preparation Plant, 18, 19, 109, 128
Newcastleton, 6, 10, 35, 36, 37, 40, 48, 57, 59, 63, 64, 72, 82, 84, 85, 90, 93, 94, 136; level crossing, 10, 37, 117; signal box, 10, 38; signalman, 37
Newcastleton Forest, 63, 136
Newtongrange, 19, 38, 46, 76, 109
Noble Grossart Limited, 47, 68, 69; rejection letter, 68
North British Hotel, 44
North British Railway, 49, 136
North British Railway Company, 43, 67, 68, 71, 73
North British Railway Study Group, 64, 76, 107, 109
North Merchiston Boys Club, 81

Oil traffic, 11, 15, 29, 38, 40, 139
On-train ticket machine, 41

Paignton-Kingswear line, 87
Parcels traffic, 54, 60, 62, 64
Parkhouse Halt, 100
Passenger traffic, 54, 60
Pate, Provost of Galashiels, 106, 107
Paterson, Alan, 9

Patillo, J, 131
Paytrain, 53
Peebles, 20, 27, 29
Peebles branch closure, 29
Peeler, Mr, 82
Pegler, Mr, 36
Penicuik, 20
Pennine Way, 107
Penny, Noel, 43, 52, 70, 75
Penton, 108
Penton House, 95
Perkins, Roy, 5, 6, 35, 40, 41, 42, 43, 45, 47, 53, 55, 56, 57, 58, 59, 61, 62, 63, 65, 69, 70, 71, 74, 75, 78, 84, 85, 90, 109, 136; archive, 36, 40, 47, 59, 68, 74, 75, 79; employment with Michelin, 35, 40
Permanent signalman, 10
Peyton, John, 83
Pick-A-Back low wagons, 64
Polton, 20
Port Carlisle branch, 49
Portobello Junction, 105
Powell-Duffryn, 63
Prescott, David, 104
Preserved locomotives of British Railways, 108
Preserved railway, 39, 41, 42, 46, 84
Proposed stations, 57, 59
Public transport interchange, 26
Radio signalling, 52

RAF Brunthill, 51, 96, 105, 114, 135
RAF Kingstown, 100
Rail network, 6
Rail tours, 48
Rails Across the Border, 9, 57
Railway Inspectorate, 52, 56
Railway Magazine, 70
Railway Observer, 107
Railway preservation, 5, 6, 45, 46
Railway solum breach, 46, 102
Railway World, 51, 52, 54, 59, 67, 70, 73, 83, 86
Railways Pocket Book No.1: Locomotives 2018, 108
Randall, Palmer & Tritton, 48
Rental from redundant buildings, 60
Reporting Scotland, 108
Reston, 30
Riccarton Junction, 37, 39, 44, 52, 63, 89, 92, 93, 119, 134, 136; signal box, 38, 91, 92, 93, 119
Riddings, 8, 38, 43, 95, 96, 107, 109, 115, 117, 136
River Eden, 105
River North Esk, 8
Road congestion, 34
Road haulage industry, 65
Road salt, 64
Road trailer, 64
Roberton, Bill, 6
Robotham, Robert, 9, 102
Rose, Major, 52
Rosewell, 20
Ross, Willie, 9
Rover Gas Turbine, 43
Roxburgh County Council, 42, 101, 102, 106, 125
Royal Bank of Scotland, 55, 56
Royal Mail, 64

Sandholm Bridge, 35
Saver tickets, 57
Science Museum, 43
Scotch Dyke, 116, 117
ScotRail, 135
Scotsman, the, 57, 72, 79, 106, 109
Scottish Borders Council, 135
Scottish Daily Express, 59

Scottish Development Department, 107
Scottish Economic Planning Board, 102
Scottish Enterprise, 64
Scottish Government, 135
Scottish Mining Museum, 19, 46
Scottish Office, 57, 82, 101, 102, 106, 109
Scottish Railway Board, 42
Scottish Railway Development Association, 62
Scottish Railway Preservation Society, 45, 46, 48, 60, 109, 115; Secretary, 46, 51
Scottish Region, British Rail, 38, 58, 65, 66, 70, 76, 80, 83, 87, 109, 117
Scottish Region: A History 1948-73, 80, 109
Scottish Trades Union Congress (TUC), 43
Secondman, 9
Secretary of State for Scotland, 9
Selkirk, 27
Selkirk Branch, 46
Settle & Carlisle line, 87, 88
Severn Valley Railway, 133
Shankend, 72, 89, 103, 115, 117, 118, 121; signal box, 38, 44, 89
Shilbottle Colliery, 139
Signal box closures, 6, 33, 37
Silloth branch, 53
Sills, Donald, 6
Simmons, Colonel, 43
Simple fare model, 57
Simpson, Mr, 47
Single-track railway, 13, 16, 20, 22, 41, 57, 59, 104, 109
Slitrig Water, 117
Smalmstown, 105
Smith, CL, 56, 78, 79
South of Scotland Chamber of Commerce, 47, 56, 85
Southern Reporter, 45
Spaven, Frank, 51, 109
Speed limit, light railways, 58
Squance, Dougie, 6 St Boswells, 11, 12, 29, 30, 31, 37, 38, 39, 40, 57, 65, 101, 102, 125, 128, 127, 132, 139, 140; goods sidings, 37, 48; oil depot, 29, 38; signal box, 31, 37, 49, 55
St Boswells – Tweedmouth line, 46, 47
St Margarets shed, 29
St Pancras, London, 10
Stainton Junction, 105
Steam tourist service, 41, 59, 63, 84, 88
Steel, David, 9, 10, 35, 44, 49, 55, 81, 103
Steele Road, 37, 93, 94
Stewart, Gordon, 66
Stewart, Leslie, 43
Stewarts Spinners, 43
Stichel Hill, 91
Stobs, 102, 117
Stoddon, Matt, 6
Stow, 15, 55, 57, 129, 132
Strang-Steel, William, 43
Strathspey Railway, 46
Sugar beet pulp, 64
Swiss railway system, 52
Symes-Schutzman, Bob, 5, 35, 40, 41, 42, 43, 45, 46, 47, 51, 52, 54, 56, 58, 60, 61, 62, 66, 67, 68, 69, 70, 71, 73, 75, 78, 80, 81, 82, 83, 85, 109
Symms, Martin, 35, 40, 41, 42, 47, 55, 56, 65, 69, 70, 78, 85; leaves project, 65

Tait, Ernest, 47, 62
Telephone and notice board, 20, 37, 38, 115
Teviot Viaduct, 34, 108, 122, 123, 134
The Great British Railway Conspiracy, 44
The line that Refused to Die, 88
The Waverley Route – the Postwar Years, 102
Thomas, John , 9

Thorpe, Willie, 70
Three Bridges, 116
Timber containerisation system, 63, 109
Timber traffic, 36, 52, 54, 63, 84, 88, 97, 103, 105, 109, 113, 139
Tomorrow's World, 35
Tornado, 98
Torwoodlee, 12
Torwoodlee Tunnel, 25
Tourist traffic, 36, 41, 54, 59, 60, 63, 84, 88
Track allocated for sale to BURCo, 70-71
Track-lifting, 5, 8, 37, 43, 47, 52, 89-100, 101, 102, 104, 107, 108, 116, 127, 129, 140; embargo, 47, 65, 71, 89, 101
Train consist, 8
Transport Scotland , 22, 135
Travelling Signalman, 13, 17, 26, 31, 38, 140
Trip E10, 7, 11, 12, 13, 14, 15, 16, 17, 18, 19, 26, 31, 37, 38, 39, 40, 44, 139
Turnbull, AM, 56
Turnbull, Norman, 6
Turner, John, 35
Tweedbank, 6, 46, 57, 59, 101, 102, 135
Tweedmouth – St Boswells line, 46, 47
Tynehead, 131

Volunteer labour, 41, 54, 84

Wauchope Forest, 136,
Waverley Association, 5, 6, 35, 42, 43, 45, 48, 52, 55, 57, 59, 61, 62, 63, 67, 70, 73, 79, 80, 81, 82, 83, 86, 87, 89, 103, 104, 111, 112; dissolution, 83; first AGM, 81, 82; Management Committee, 60; new Scottish Management Committee, 81, 82, 83; Passenger Users Survey, 60; questionaire, 80; relationship with BURCo, 6, 43, 54, 61, 67, 73, 74; Secretary, 35, 42, 43, 56, 79, 86
Waverley Line Action Group, 47
Waverley Route, 5, 6, 7, 8, 9, 10, 11, 17, 18, 19, 23, 25, 26, 27, 32, 35, 37, 38, 39, 40, 43, 44, 48, 50, 51, 52, 56, 58, 59, 64, 65, 68, 69, 70, 80, 81, 83, 85, 89, 95, 100, 102, 103, 104, 105, 106, 107, 108, 109, 115, 116, 125, 136; campaign against closure, 9, 10; campaign for reopening, 9; condition at closure, 55; diversionary route for WCML, 103, 104, 105, 113;final protest against closure, 10, 48, 54, 117; last revenue producing train, 17, 49; last steam-hauled service, 98; retention of Edinburgh-Hawick section, 8, 9, 88; signalling, 37
Waverley Route Heritage Centre, 39
Waverley Route Trust, 135
Waverley Route: the battle for the Borders Railway, 9, 39, 51, 132, 135
Waverley Route: the life, death and rebirth of the Borders Railway, 5, 6
Weardale Railway, 84
Weighell, Sid, 54
Wellington Arms, Woolwich, 35
West Coast Main Line, 44, 50, 51, 52, 69, 115, 117; electrification, 103, 104, 105
West Coast Railways, 108
West Somerset Railway, 84
Wheatland Road, 107
White, HP, 10
Whitehouse, Alan, 88
Whitrope, 39, 44, 90, 138; siding, 37; summit, 91; tunnel, 44, 90, 107, 114
Wolfe, Professor, 57
Workington, 63

York, 71
Young, Allan, 6
Younger, George, 82